FOR DEVE

Development Matters

Development Matters is a series of comprehensive but concise introductions to the key issues in development studies. It offers politically engaged and challenging critiques while demonstrating academic and conceptual rigour to provide readers with critical, reflexive and challenging explorations of the pressing concerns in development. With carefully designed features, such as explanatory text boxes, glossaries and recommended reading, the series provides the reader with accessible guides to development studies.

Series Editors
Helen Yanacopulos and Matt Baillie Smith

Titles already published
Bjorn Hettne, *Thinking about Development*
James Smith, *Science and Technology for Development*

About the authors

Hazel Johnson is Professor of Development Policy and Practice at the Open University, UK.

Gordon Wilson is Senior Lecturer in Technology and Development at the Open University, UK.

LEARNING
FOR DEVELOPMENT

DEVELOPMENT **MATTERS**

HAZEL JOHNSON AND GORDON WILSON

Zed Books
London & New York

Learning for Development was first published in 2009 by Zed Books
Ltd, 7 Cynthia Street, London N1 9JF, UK and Room 400, 175 Fifth
Avenue, New York, NY 10010, USA

www.zedbooks.co.uk

FSC
Mixed Sources
Product group from well-managed
forests and other controlled sources
Cert no. SGS-COC-2953
www.fsc.org
© 1996 Forest Stewardship Council

Designed and typeset by Kate Kirkwood
Index by John Barker
Cover designed by Rogue Four Design
Printed and bound in Great Britain by CPI Antony
Rowe, Chippenham and Eastbourne

Distributed in the USA exclusively by Palgrave Macmillan, a division of
St Martin's Press, LLC, 175 Fifth Avenue, New York, NY 10010, USA

A catalogue record for this book is available from the British Library
Library of Congress Cataloging in Publication Data available

ISBN 978 1 84813 197 2 hb
ISBN 978 1 84813 198 9 pb
ISBN 978 1 84813 199 6 eb

Contents

Acknowledgements

Many people have contributed to the research that we have written about in this book. In particular we would like to thank all the people who collaborated in being interviewed, engaged with all our questions, and provided us with information. They are too many to list here, but without their collegiality this work would have been impossible.

We would also like to thank co-researchers who worked with us on particular studies: Gabi Haiss and Charlene Hewatt without whom we would not have been able to carry out the multiple stakeholder research in Zimbabwe (Chapter 3); and the team involved in the research project on Education for Development Policy and Management (EDPM) in the UK and East and Southern Africa (Chapter 5): Seife Ayele, Peter Dzvimbo, Patricia Kasiamhuru, Joyce Malaba, Pauline Manjengwa, Florence Nazare, Herman Potgieter, Alan Thomas, Sheila Tyler and Alan Woodley. We would also like to thank the Department for International Development for providing funding for the EDPM research.

1 | Why Learning for Development?

This book in the *Development Matters* series takes a learning approach to development. The focus is on the everyday learning that takes place through development action, which may be intentional and structured as well as informal and an outcome of different forms of engagement. The social dynamics of learning are important for individuals, for their organizations and for building coherent policy and action. The connection between these processes is not straightforward – the organizational and institutional embedding of new learning is often one of the biggest challenges for development, and is a recurring theme throughout the book. This first chapter engages with the considerable scope of the field, and outlines our approach.

Conceptualizing a learning approach to development

Contemporary development theorist Jan Nederveen Pieterse defines development 'as the organized intervention in collective affairs according to a standard of improvement. What constitutes improvement and what is appropriate intervention obviously vary according to class, culture, historical context and relations of power' (2001: 3). This definition is purposive: development involves deliberate action to bring about positive changes for humanity. Nederveen Pieterse does signal, however, that both purpose and process are contested arenas.

The contested nature of defining development and of what

constitute 'organized intervention' and 'standard of improvement' is also present in the three views of development outlined by Thomas (2000). Starting with the notion of development as 'good change' put forward by Chambers (1997), Thomas notes first that development is a vision of a particular state of being. There are many visions of being, however, and such differences will be socially and culturally defined as well as changing over time and having different representations in different historical periods and parts of the world. Second, development is seen as a historical process: the dynamics of social, political and economic organization as they have changed over time – particularly, but not only, within capitalism. There are different analyses and interpretations of this historical process, and especially of the nature of capitalist development, with its historical links to colonialism and access to cheap inputs for industrialization from different parts of the world. Third, development is intentional activity: the interventions of different actors (state and non-state) deliberately taken to bring about what those actors consider to be 'good change'. Again, what is considered to be 'good change' will be informed by different understandings of development and will hence be supported by different policies and approaches to intervention.

There are obvious similarities between Nederveen Pieterse's 'organized intervention' and Thomas's intentional development, and his 'standard of improvement' is associated with a vision of a desirable state of being. However, development as a historical process is fundamental to the other two conceptions: by studying history, we gain a sense of why development has occurred in particular ways in different parts of the world – outcomes which include, of course, both the inexorable process of change in social, economic and political conditions, and the actions and interventions of those who wished deliberately to bring about change with the intention of improving well-being as a whole. Those actions, in history as in the present, have been informed by visions and perspectives about what constitutes development (even if 'development' was not the terminology used). Indeed it has been suggested by Cowen and Shenton that development in its modern form was conceived in response to the negative effects of capitalism in the early nineteenth century, and that 'to develop . . . was to ameliorate the social misery which arose out of the immanent process of capitalist growth' (1996: 116). Since then, the main 'big debate' has been whether development should take place alongside capitalism or should envisage another social order. More recently, 'another social order' – in terms of its representation in socialism and communism – is seen as having failed, with some exceptions, such as in Cuba and China, although changes in those economies – particularly in China – have challenged their original Marxist visions. However, development alongside capitalism has also been judged by many as having failed the large majority of poor people (in spite of massive changes in South-East Asia and in the BRICS).[1] In the views of different structuralist and post-development thinkers, in particular, the development alongside capitalism 'project' is seen as the cause of the lack of development or underdevelopment in certain parts of the world (and as responsible for poverty and inequality within advanced capitalist societies).

Such contestations in terms of big ideas about the social order have been reflected in theoretical debates about development, whether in terms of grand theory about the nature of capitalist and socialist development, or with respect to middle-level theories of alternative and people-centred human development. Apart from currents of Marxism and post-development thinkers, most theorizing of development has been aligned to greater or lesser extents with policy and intervention within or alongside capitalism. Alternative development and human development thinkers have challenged capitalism in terms of its negative impacts and have argued for the need to focus on human needs, social and community development, human capabilities and democracy. Although it can be debated whether such ideas constitute the basis of a completely different social form, they have certainly challenged the neo-liberal currents and capitalist growth orthodoxies of the 1980s. The theories of development that under-lie the alternative and human development visions have also been closely linked in turn to approaches that promote participation, empowerment and capacity building, which have influenced major institutions such as the World Bank in their studies of the 'voices of the poor'.[2] As Thomas notes (2000: 20–1), even post-development thinkers have acknowledged the need for action, although with the strong caveat that interveners should 'start examining the whys and wherefores of their actions' (Rahnema, 1997: 397).

This book focuses on intentional development while arguing that the actions of interveners are fundamentally part of, and contribute to, development as history. Intentional development includes actors who may be considered as having 'trusteeship': 'the intent which is expressed, by one source of agency, to develop the capacities of another' (Cowen and Shenton, 1996: x). For example, our case studies include those working in non-governmental organizations (NGOs), those in local government in North and South, and development managers who might be working in many types of organization. What legitimacy such trustees of development have, for whom, and for what are of course questions that need to be answered – rather more for NGOs and other development organizations, perhaps, than for democratically constituted local government. However, inten-tional development includes many forms of organization in the public sphere, such as social movements and campaigning organizations whose sources of legitimacy, types of trusteeship and purposes may be very different from those of entities such as NGOs and government institutions.

Because of the multiplicity of actors in development and of orga-nizational forms, we prefer to use the term *development action* rather than intentional development. The concept of development action is akin to the notion of public action as discussed by Drèze and Sen (1989), Mackintosh (1992) and Wuyts (1992): 'purpo-sive collective action, whether for collective private ends or for public ends' (Mackintosh, 1992: 5). It goes without saying that development action, as public action, can be informed by many different visions, histories, contexts or interests, and can have a wide range of means at its disposal.

Acknowledging that development is potentially a struggle between conflicting analyses, interests and policies, we suggest that the post-development exhortation to examine the whys and wherefores of action is fundamental. We also argue that such an examination is key to learning through and for development action, without underestimating the challenge posed. For example, Nederveen Pieterse (2001) argues that development should be reflexive, that development thinking *is* reflexive by its very nature, and that the global changes of recent times compel us to adopt such an approach. Such changes include:

- new understandings of the dynamics of development – the importance of the 'software' (institutions, education and knowledge) as well as the 'hardware' (infrastructure and technology);
- the massive growth in actors in development, from the state to community organizations: 'development is no longer simply a mathematics of power and reshuffling the status quo' (*ibid.*: 157);
- an increase in the influence of Southern perspectives in development; and economic convergence, in particular the growth of the newly industrializing countries and the BRICS.

Such changes, Nederveen Pieterse argues, require us to re-define development 'as a collective learning experience' (*ibid.*: 159) involving collective reflexivity: 'a collective awareness that unfolds as part of a historical process of changing norms, ideologies and institutions' (*ibid.*: 163).

To these elements we would add an important dimension to collective learning: the information revolution and the enormous changes that information and communication technologies have made to connections between actors in different parts of the world. This in turn has underlined the role of knowledge in development, extolled by the World Bank (1998), an emphasis that led to the creation of a 'Knowledge Bank'. However, the relationship between information and knowledge; how they are generated and shaped (and for what purpose); their links to global power relations and policy formation; and their role in learning – are all issues for debate. Samoff and Stromquist argue that 'distilled and digested bits of information disseminated through Internet websites risk perpetuating rather than reducing dependence. . . . What is needed is learning, largely initiated, maintained, managed, and sustained by those seeking to change their situation' (Samoff and Stromquist, 2001: 654).

In sharing such a perspective, we argue that a crucial dimension of development action is social engagement. But what kind of social engagement? For example, one emergent school of thought at the start of the new millennium has taken a critical perspective on the idea of 'participation', which has informed the theory and practice of much development action. An alternative idea of active or radical citizenship is proposed (Mohan and Hickey, 2004). However it is unrealistic to expect that there will be continual engagement of this kind (even though some forms of action will undoubtedly align themselves to social currents, campaigns and movements). The everyday dimensions of development action demand a socially aware and reflexive pragmatism as well as active citizenship, not least because much development action takes the form of defined projects, which are often short-term and circumscribed by funding agencies with particular interests. Their ubiquity leads us to refer to the 'projectization' of development action. However whether development action takes place through ongoing active citizenship and/or development projects (note that development projects could also be an expression of active citizenship), social engagement is likely to be characterized by conflicting perspectives, values and goals. For such social engagement to have longer-term and positive impact, reflexive learning, negotiation and accommodation are needed.

Even so, as Nederveen Pieterse points out, collective and

reflexive learning cannot assume that those in positions of power will engage to make the world a more equal place. Collective action is also needed (2001:163). Collective action can take many forms, from collaboration and cooperation across apparently conflicting or disparate interests, to campaigning for fundamental social change. Collective action can create the space for collective learning. Collective learning in turn requires acknowledging and validating difference, and, as we will see from case studies in this book, establishing trust (Chapter 4). It may be difficult or even impossible to build trust in contexts of inequality and unequal power. Nevertheless, learning can also take place through conflict (Chapter 3), as well as through making mistakes (Chapters 3, 4 and 6; see also Chambers, 1997).

Learning for development has had many points of focus – outlined in what follows as we preview the contents of this book.

The scope of learning for development

Historically, much of the literature on learning in and for development has examined learning as part of immanent development, or development as a historical process. This focus particularly applies to analyses of industrialization, about which there is a substantial literature on technology transfer, technological learning and learning from the experience of others. This literature often focuses on models of development (for example, East Asian models), and whether such models are replicable in other parts of the world.

Building models is one way of sharing and communicating learning. There are, however, different ways of conceptualizing models. One way is as a blueprint that might suggest how something can be done. There is a tendency to be sceptical about blueprints because success and failure may be highly dependent on the particular features of a given context. However blueprints can also be useful in very similar situations. On the other hand, using models as points of comparison rather than replication is a useful learning tool to inform policy and action. Using models for learning can be a powerful mechanism to decide what to change, adapt or use directly – as well as what not to do. Such processes have been strongly advocated by more systemic and holistic views of how learning takes place and how it can be sustained over time (Korten, 1992; Rondinelli, 1993; Clark *et al.*, 2003).

One blueprint that has pervaded development projects (as opposed to other kinds of development action) relates to one of the tools and techniques of development that is presumed to promote learning. This is 'project cycle management', which involves identifying needs and objectives, planning and implementation, and assessment of outcomes. Learning is expected to take place (through monitoring and evaluation) throughout the cycle; it is assumed that the process will adjust to new events or changes in context, as well as gaining from past experience. A particular tool in project cycle management is 'logical framework analysis' (or LFA), which provides a matrix for relating a hierarchy of activities to overall goals with measures and indicators of success. During this process the assumptions underlying the activities and goals are made explicit. LFA is deemed to have learning embedded within it, as actors can evaluate their performance against their progress through the logical framework. The underlying assumptions are crucially important, as they may determine whether outcomes are achieved or not; checking out assumptions is thus a very important part of the learning process.

Such approaches have also been subject to criticism. One criticism of LFA is its overriding concern with accountability, reflecting an audit culture that seeks to reduce uncertainty to measurable goals. As Gasper notes, such processes are limited in usefulness when there are unintended effects, when interactions are complex, and if there are major differences between stakeholders (2000: 27). Other writers concur. For example, Biggs and Smith (2003) argue that project cycle management, assumed to promote learning, has taken primacy over organizational settings and cultures and usurped the place of human agency, which can fundamentally influence development programmes and projects. Indeed, Clark *et al.* would argue that individual actors, even more than organizations, can have a catalytic influence over the outcomes of development action (2003: 1859).

Alternative approaches, developed by the International Development Research Centre in Canada (IDRC), have focused on 'outcome mapping' in response to the perceived rigidities of logical framework analysis. IDRC notes:

> LFA takes a 'mechanistic' view focusing on the 'ballistic' term 'impact' which implies a discrete, measurable, predictable and straightforward relationship between a programme and the change it wishes to make, whereas OM [outcome mapping] sees development as characterized by long-term, open problems, and recognizes that social change is complex and requires change in many actors over a long period of time. Following from this, LFA assumes that the results development programmes aim for are fully within their control, whereas OM is based on an understanding that agencies can only influence and contribute to development outcomes. (IDRC, 2007: 7)

Such reflections, particularly those about organizational and cultural settings and the role of human agency, take us back to social engagement and active citizenship as points of learning. To put this in context, there is debate over whether interveners (for example, professionals working in development) are perpetuating a neo-colonial form of development administration, or whether they are providing avenues for new kinds of approaches and engagement (Cooke, 2003; Kothari, 2005) – something that we pick up on at different points in this book. There is no easy answer to this question. On one hand, development professionals work within the paradigms and accepted wisdom of their own social settings, even though they may seek to gain awareness of other social settings and to act in a reflexive way – that is, being conscious of and reflecting on their own actions. On the other hand, development professionals also work within powerful institutional and organizational agendas that may be difficult to contest

(Borda-Rodriguez, 2008). An important issue, then, is whether different actors and stakeholders in development action are able to transcend power-based agendas and join in a shared language of open engagement. Such a process, of course, involves trust.

The importance of trust for effective relationships through which actors can learn is well known. However, the rhetoric of trust, which is often accompanied by the rhetoric of mutuality between stakeholders, can disguise deeper inequalities and divisions. This point has often been raised with respect to the role of partnership in development, a mantra of many governments and one of the Millennium Development Goals for 2015. As noted by Noxolo, when commenting on the importance given to partnership in a UK 1997 White Paper on development, 'mutuality in Britain's international relationships would imply an acknowledgement of the agency of both Britain *and* of other post-colonial countries' (2006: 264, emphasis in original). Keeping the 'whys and wherefores' of development action in mind is thus essential, including an understanding and proper appreciation of the agency of those characterized by Samoff and Stromquist above as 'seeking to change their situation'.

Yet it is through social engagement that potential inequalities and limited perspectives on development can be challenged – and trust can be built. This point is addressed by one of the authors of this book in an examination of the role of professional expertise in development. Wilson suggests that there is potential for learning in engagements between experts and citizens, if there is a basis of shared values. While trust can develop from shared values, Wilson also suggests that 'the very process of engaging in joint practice can develop trust' (2006: 519). However trust building has a number of requirements, some of which we explore in this book. It can also take time. As Clark *et al.* note from their own case study of using research to build capacities in post-harvest innovation in India, relationships 'were built on trust, shared values and perspectives, some of which had been built up over a long period before the project' (2003: 1859).

To build trust through joint action, and to enable learning through building trust, is potentially to complete a virtuous and continuous circle. Such engagement, which includes 'learning with' as well as 'learning from' experts, can create a 'learning space' (Wilson, 2006) – an opportunity resulting from social interaction for new learning. The learning demonstrated in the case studies in this book is both 'learning with' and 'learning from'. We do not deny the importance of the latter – different processes are needed, and different kinds of learning. However, to encapsulate the importance of social engagement in learning, we also add 'action' to the concept of learning space (Johnson, 2007) – that is, the creation of opportunities for learning through joint action, and the interaction of codified (written) and tacit (within a person or group) knowledge in everyday practice. This view chimes with Samoff's and Stromquist's critique of online knowledge building. Although the information and knowledge revolution has provided huge opportunities for dissemination, and potentially for learning, we concur with these authors that 'using knowledge to solve problems and overcome obstacles is necessarily an active process in which the problem solvers must be directly involved in generating the knowledge they require' (2001: 654).

The structure of this book

Rather than attempting to cover the vast field touched on above, this book uses the results of a series of small research projects that we have carried out over nearly ten years to examine different types of learning for development. We first discuss some key ideas, concepts and issues in learning and the production of knowledge for development, in particular the social nature of learning (and the dynamics of learning in social groups and organizations), as well as the challenges of power, inequality and democratic engagement. In Chapter 3, we examine the experience of a multi-stakeholder intervention in Zimbabwe, and the role of challenging assumptions and contestation in learning about the interests and concerns of stakeholder groups. Chapter 4, by contrast, analyses the experience of two North–South municipal partnerships whose rationale was practitioner-to-practitioner learning, and examines the nature of peer engagement across different social histories and cultures. In Chapter 5, we consider the experiences of development managers who engage with formal learning processes, and the impact of their learning on their own perceptions and practices, as well as on their organizations. Chapter 6 focuses on a pilot project to test the potential of using online communication to promote learning for different types of actor in the public sphere, and the social and technical challenges of such an experiment. Our final chapter reflects on theoretical and empirical insights from the case studies, in particular in relation to development action as a reflexive practice and the creation and use of action learning spaces.

Notes

1 Brazil, Russia, India, China and South Africa have all experienced considerable economic change and growth in the early years of the twenty-first century (hence the acronym, BRICS).
2 The title of the three-volume World Bank study carried out in the 1990s, which informed the 2000 World Bank report *Attacking Poverty*. This report documented the changed approach of the World Bank since its 1990 report, which had emphasized labour intensity, investment in human capital and social safety nets as the means to poverty reduction. The new emphasis was on opportunity, security and empowerment.

2 | Approaches to Learning for Development

In this chapter, we outline some ways of approaching learning for development and issues that they raise. As noted in Chapter 1, learning and knowledge for development are growing areas of study and practice. There is now an extensive arena of debate that addresses concepts as well as tools, techniques and skills for promoting learning, knowledge sharing and knowledge management in development. Discussion in this chapter, however, is not about tools, techniques and skills. Rather the approaches we consider focus on several underlying ideas and concepts – for example, power and communicative action (see the discussion of this concept below) – within the broader, but closely related, arenas of knowledge and ways of understanding the social dynamics of learning.

We group these different approaches into three areas of concern that broadly relate to the conceptions of development outlined in Chapter 1 – though these conceptions are not neatly distinct categories. The first area of concern is with understanding *how and why learning occurs*. In part, this concern is strongly related to development as history – the processes through which change occurs and the incentives for actors (particularly small to large enterprises, whether public or private) to learn from each other, to create new products, processes and markets, and to generate wealth. Much of the debate has been on technological learning and innovation, although more recent writing has focused on institutions and systems within which learning and innovation take place (or to which learning and innovation give rise). It would be a mistake, however, to think that such learning and innovation are simply emergent processes – they are often also planned, deliberate actions designed to bring about particular kinds of change. Institutions such as the World Bank, the United Nations Industrial Development Organization, the World Trade Organization and the International Labour Organization are all interested in enterprise innovation for development and its impacts on economic, particularly industrial, growth, trade and employment.

Other writers on 'how learning occurs' examine development interventions specifically. Learning may emerge from those interventions or the interventions may themselves have been designed with the purpose of promoting learning. These types of learning are an important part of this book and we will be considering some of the ideas that have been used to frame and understand them below.

Into our second group fall concerns with *how to promote learning* for development: the ideas, frameworks, tools, techniques and skills that aim to achieve learning between actors (whether they are government bodies, enterprises, development organizations, community groups or individuals). Such processes are usually directed at building capacities and capabilities, on one hand, and increasing the impact and scope of development activity on the other. Debates in this area are closely aligned to intentional development and have spawned an extensive set of books, articles, manuals and accounts of experiences.

With respect to building capacities and capabilities, some writers have focused on what are called 'learning process approaches' to development. The concept of a learning process approach has been used by David Korten (1992) to specify a particular, staged process to supporting learning in development interventions, but it also denotes a range of approaches which attempt to promote such learning (see, for example, Rondinelli, 1993; Wijayaratna and Uphoff, 1997). Building capacities and capabilities is also associated with participatory approaches to

Learning and participation

Learning process approaches allow subjects of development and development professionals to share their knowledge and resources in creating a programme which achieves a fit between the needs and capacities of the beneficiaries and those of the outsiders who are providing the assistance. Research and action are integrally linked (adapted from Korten, 1980: 497).

The stages of learning process approaches

Learning to be effective
Learning to be efficient
Learning to expand
(*Ibid.*: 499–500)

Participatory approaches to development

'Participatory development is conventionally represented as emerging out of the recognition of the shortcomings of top-down development approaches' (Cooke and Kothari, 2001b: 5). Participatory approaches to development aim 'to make "people" central to development by encouraging beneficiary involvement in interventions that affect them and over which they previously had limited control or influence' (*ibid.*).

This large family of approaches includes Participatory Rural Appraisal (PRA) and Participatory Learning and Action (PLA). PRA involves enabling rural people to share and analyse knowledge to be able to take action and learn from it (Chambers, 1997: 104). PLA broadly encompasses PRA and other approaches to promote what it says: participatory learning and action. So it focuses on learning by all participants, acknowledges and aims to understand diversity, involves group interaction and analysis, addresses specific contexts, often uses external facilitation, and leads to proposals to bring about change (Pretty *et al.*, 1995: 56–7).

development. The concept of participation has a particular idea about learning at its core, namely that 'experts' in development should listen to and learn from the knowledge and ideas of those who are the subjects of intervention rather than the other way round – or 'putting the last first ' (Chambers, 1997). Writings on participatory approaches include an ever-increasing range of manuals, websites and tools (for example, Participatory Rural Appraisal, Participatory Learning and Action) and techniques (for example, buzz groups, wealth ranking and diagramming) for promoting the participation of actors in development.

More generally, participatory learning approaches have had a strong influence on how we think about intentional development. They have also been a subject of critical scrutiny, which we come back to in Chapter 3.

Many of these debates and the types of action associated with them are a riposte to a long history of ideas about knowledge transfer in development and conventional approaches to technical assistance and training. It is argued that these earlier approaches, which tend to see learning as linear rather than iterative and interactive, have simply served to perpetuate the status of experts and expert knowledge; they have promoted dependent cultures of assumed ignorance and have failed to build dynamic and positive processes of shared learning and knowledge production that benefit poor people.

Criticism of linear approaches to learning and knowledge transfer have also given rise to processes and techniques for promoting knowledge sharing (for example, open space sessions, knowledge fairs, Dgroups and different types of peer-to-peer engagement – see box opposite). They are represented in practice-based journals, websites, discussion fora and the promotion of 'communities of practice' (to which we return below). Knowledge sharing has been advocated and promoted by major institutions such as the World Bank Institute, and the United Nations Development Programme, for use within these organiszations as well as to provide online platforms for knowledge sharing on an international basis. There are now numerous such online platforms and fora, as well as growing scrutiny of their use, impact and effectiveness. Many development organizations have recognized the importance of knowledge for development and have explicit programmes to promote knowledge sharing and knowledge management (King and McGrath, 2004). In Chapter 1, we mentioned an early critical study (Samoff and Stromquist, 2001).

Sharing knowledge

Open space sessions enable people with common interests or a common topic of concern to come together for discussion.

Knowledge fairs showcase information/knowledge about a particular topic, theme, debate, organization, institution, *et cetera*. They frequently include speakers, displays, and audio-visual presentations, and enable people to interact with presenters.

Dgroups: Development through Dialogue – a non-commercial, low-bandwidth, electronic platform that offers services to bring groups together.[1]

Our third group of concerns is about *learning for what purpose?* This group parallels the idea of development as a vision. Visions of development are highly contested, however, and influenced by different values, interests, norms and cultures. Thus trying to achieve a particular vision of development has to address power relations, dominant political and economic interests, and access to and control over ideas, knowledge and development technologies. Writers who address such issues are therefore concerned with the obstacles to inclusive, collective learning, and to knowledge sharing, and include those with a strong critique of some of the current perspectives on development. They include those who question how development is conceptualized (for example, Crush, 1995; Rahnema and Bawtree, 1997) and how it is achieved (for example, the critique of participation by Cooke and Kothari, 2001b; Hickey and Mohan, 2004).

The importance of these currents of thinking lies in their focus on social relations between actors, particularly power relations. As we will see below and in the following chapters, power and other social relations, however explicit or embedded, are fundamental to how and whether learning for development occurs, what kind of learning, and for what purpose. Thus, as we have seen, the critique of participation, although it does not address learning directly, proposes a vision of active and radical citizenship through which learning for a different kind of development can take place.

The following sections of this chapter draw on these three areas of concern, which also run through the rest of the book. Underlying them are ideas about how and why human beings communicate and what they communicate about; how learning is mediated by dominant 'truths' (for example, about development); and how learning proceeds from difference between people and between their social worlds, on one hand, while simultaneously being situated in or emerging from particular social and temporal contexts, on the other. In the final section of the chapter, we outline our own concept of 'action learning space' which we use at different points in the book.

Learning through reflection and communication within a framework of truth

This section considers the work of two of the most influential social philosophers in the second half of the twentieth century: Jürgen Habermas (1929–) and Michel Foucault (1926–84). These are by no means the only thinkers who have written about issues of power, knowledge and social change: Bourdieu's notion of 'habitus' which Borda-Rodriguez (2008) characterizes as an internalized set of expectations arising from knowledge of past experiences, and Latour's actor-network theory come immediately to mind (Latour, 2005). However, neither explores the philosophical basis of the complex social dynamics of learning and knowledge production through social engagement which is the concern of Habermas, nor the interconnections between micro-level knowledge produced through social engagements and framing macro-knowledges (or 'truths') of Foucault.

Using Habermas and Foucault together is unusual as they were often at odds with one another, basically over the former's fundamental attachment to the possibility of rational discussion which can lead to political emancipation of the oppressed (Edgar, 2006: 114). There are, however, sound reasons for focusing on them in this book.

First, as we shall see, Habermas's theory of communicative action resonates strongly with social theories of learning, social learning for development (as outlined in Chapter 1), and with the discussion of knowledge sharing above. Moreover communicative action also resonates with development thinking around participatory approaches to learning, knowledge and action.

Second, as implied above, Foucault's analysis of how societal 'truths' are produced, perpetuated and challenged provides a useful analytical tool for thinking about the framing of knowledge–power contexts in which social learning is embedded.

Finally, taken together, the ideas of Habermas and Foucault encapsulate the tension between the potential for active social agency to lead to emancipatory/transformative learning (see below) and the constraining macro-knowledge frameworks within which such agency operates. Drawing on the same thinkers, Borda-Rodriguez has also explored this tension, which he categorizes as the extent to which (1) development knowledge is framed and its practitioners are constrained by a macro-level dominant discourse and by meso-level discourses of international development organizations; and (2) there is potential at a micro-level of engagement between actors for fruitful knowledge exchange and production, despite the constraining influence of these discourses (2008: 13).

Here it should be noted that Habermas and Foucault both wrote extensively about knowledge rather than learning but, given the intimate relationship between the two concepts,[2] their work is highly relevant for this book.

Instrumental and communicative learning

What is the primary distinguishing feature that makes us human? This simple question is the driving force behind Habermas's work.[3] His answer: our capacity to reflect on what we do and learn. Habermas then argues that this fundamental capacity, which is present in all human beings, is the source of two capabilities (Edgar, 2006: 62–4):

- Our ability to 'labour', by which Habermas means our ability to transform our physical environment or 'nature' for productive use.
- Our ability to interact and communicate with each other, not just in the sense of conveying information, but to justify our reflections in the form of discussion, debate and challenge.

Habermas is certainly not the first person to refer explicitly to the first of these capabilities. In the nineteenth century, for example, the ability to labour formed the underlying assumption in the work of Karl Marx. Habermas himself belongs to a neo-Marxist school of thought, but he does offer a critique of 'classical' Marx which concerns the latter's neglect of the second capability above. Habermas argues that, for Marx, our ability to transform the physical environment drives everything we do – the organization of production and capitalist society and hence social change. However Habermas insists that the form in which change takes place is not pre-ordained and that the mechanism by which we change society is our communicative ability (*ibid.*).

This debate between the ideas of Habermas and Marx can be

used to inform our first area of concern: how and why learning for development occurs. Thomas's sense of development as historical process refers explicitly to the propensity of capitalism to build on itself in a cyclical or immanent process (2000: 29). Market competition that is inherent to capitalism drives technological innovation, which in turn creates both (new) products and processes. This immanent process assumes, however, that we have the ability to engage in technological innovation, which in turn depends on our evolving new knowledge through reflection and communication, in other words through learning. Indeed, technological innovation may be defined as knowledge for productive use (Ayele and Wield, 2005). It is a knowledge that is linked to our fundamental ability to labour – that is, to transform 'nature' – and we learn that new knowledge through, and because of, the dynamic of capitalism.

The three interests of knowledge

Habermas posits three interests of knowledge. These are summarized by Mohan and Wilson (2005) as:

Technical – aimed at the material reproduction of society and how one controls and manipulates one's environment (instrumentalism). This is largely based on *scientific* approaches.

Hermeneutic – aimed at enhancing understanding and transforming consciousness through binding consensual norms. This is largely based on approaches whereby communication and intersubjectivity allow a greater *understanding* of meanings of the social worlds we inhabit.

Emancipatory – aimed at breaking free from structures which limit our options and which have hitherto been regarded as beyond human control. This involves critical *self-reflection* through which people can truly recognize the source of their problems.

Habermas would take issue with this description of development as historical process, however, because he thinks that it reduces human ability for reflection and creativity to a *technical* interest of knowledge and communication (see box on previous page). Important as this is, crucially it ignores the human ability to (1) reflect on society, and interpret it through discussion, challenge and debate with others (what he calls a *hermeneutic interest*); and (2) challenge and shape that society (an *emancipatory interest*). Habermas's division of knowledge into technical, hermeneutic and emancipatory interests is the most-quoted aspect of his work (Habermas, 1987a).

The issue, therefore, is not that the idea of development as historical process as articulated by Thomas is wrong, but that it leaves something out. We don't only reflect and communicate in order to drive capitalism onwards. The structural inequalities associated with capitalism, along with other impacts, both positive and negative, also generate wider, immanent processes of reflection and communication in the social sphere and it is this that drives social change. Nevertheless, one can also challenge a certain optimism in Habermas. Because of capitalism's economic, political and ideological dominance it tends to be conflated with reality. In other words, it constitutes the 'truth' of how the world functions which frames what might be learned, and is undoubtedly a constraining force on the generation of alternative knowledges that might challenge it. The universal 'truth' of capitalism thus appears to make fanciful any notion of development knowledge beyond doing capitalism better.

Habermas (1984: 143–242) himself has grappled with this issue that he calls *instrumental rationality,* which privileges technical knowledge and concerns exchanges of information gaining precedence over *communicative rationality*, which might breed challenge to the social system (see also Borda-Rodriguez, 2008: 42–3). He doesn't, however, reject instrumental rationality as such, recognizing that it is essential for societies to function. For him, and for us, the key issue is the way that instrumental rationality

---

Instrumental vs communicative rationality

Instrumental rationality is summarized by Edgar (2006: 74) as the rational choice for the achievement of any given end. It is thus a rationality associated with selection of means rather than of ends. Instrumental rationality is fundamental, for example, to the application of technology, judged by its efficiency and effectiveness, as well as in social administration and in the formation of social and economic policies.

Communicative rationality and communicative action. In contrast to instrumental rationality, communicative rationality concerns the rational choice of ends, arrived at by communicative action — free and open discussion of all relevant persons without any form of coercion (Edgar, 2006: 23).

---

has a tendency to build on itself with the evolution of society, and is in danger of eclipsing communicative rationality in a process that he calls the 'colonization of the lifeworld' (*ibid*.; Habermas, 1987b). This does not bode well for learning that is emancipatory, which comes about through discussion, debate and challenge – in short a process which he calls *communicative action* (*ibid*.).

Thus how and why learning occurs cannot be divorced from the kind of learning and the knowledge it produces, which leads to the second concern about how to promote learning, in this instance in the context of development intervention – a crucial element of which has always been increasing the stock of knowledge. In the early days after the Second World War, it was largely conceived as technical assistance. Although the term survives today, especially in World Bank and IMF circles, others now conceive knowledge for development in terms of capacity building (Wilson, 2007). Technical assistance, as the name implies, was overtly instrumental in conception. Essentially, it embodied how the Western world does things and manages its affairs. This knowledge was to be transferred to the unknowing South and was not open to question.

Development knowledge as capacity building since the mid-1990s represents an attempt to move away from the instrumentalism associated with technical assistance. As such it is strongly associated with participatory approaches to development intervention, to which we have referred above.

In its rhetoric, participation seems akin to Habermas's *ideal speech situation* (1990: 88). This is also known as an *unrestricted communication community*, following Apel (1980): a deliberate attempt to create the conditions for free and transparent communication among all stakeholders in an intervention. But participation has also been accused of instrumentalism (see, for example, Cleaver, 1999) – a means of learning or self-discovery of capitalist 'truths' (Wilson, 2006) where possibilities for transformative (or emancipatory) knowledge creation become undermined.

The participation debate points towards a difficult issue for the Habermasian notion of communicative action. To the extent that development intervention is required to have a positive impact on those at whom it is directed, this can only be achieved through a significant degree of instrumentality. Assumptions have to be made, such as that capitalism is the way the world is, or, at a more mundane level, predicting with reasonable certainty how other stakeholders (whether individuals or partner organizations) will react to proposals. Just in order to get jobs done, it is often impossible to think about, let alone participate in, open and transparent communication with others, except perhaps in the most minimalist of interpretations. Take the following quotation from a development manager:

> On days like this (and there are so many), I am left thinking, how it is possible to suit or meet community needs, and to be acceptable to them, at the same time as trying to retain reputation from

outsiders such as donors? Or are we just using such communities for our own learning . . . while poor villagers are left off helpless . . . with lots of semantic and sweeping statements. . . . The list of catchphrases includes participation, democratic process, working partnership, decentralization. But does it end up with grassroots people with access to decision-making machinery . . . or . . . are they still dictated to by the facilitators? On a day like this you are faced with people's immediate problems but have to conduct PRA [Participatory Rural Appraisal]. You talk about flexibility but have to worry because your year's schedule must be modified because the roads are inaccessible. (Crawford *et al.*, 1999: 173)

Habermas is well aware of this tension between instrumental and communicative rationality, as indicated above. There are, however, two further issues that arise, even when the space is allowed for open and transparent discussion in development intervention. For Habermas, a precondition for communicative exchange is that the participants are able to draw on assumptions that are held in common, mutually drawing on a shared *lifeworld*

Lifeworlds

A *lifeworld* is the stock of competences and knowledge that people use to negotiate their way through everyday life, to interact with others, and ultimately to create and maintain social relationships (Edgar, 2006: 89). Our lifeworld competences make communicative action possible (see box on page 23). They typically are used to maintain our relationships with people we know, not only through taken-for-granted agreement, but also through challenge and negotiation. The interactions involved, however, require that we establish a basic shared view of the way the world works through establishing common meanings and common interpretations of the lifeworld (*ibid.*: 90). In other words, we establish a *shared* lifeworld or background consensus.

(Habermas, 1984, 1987b, 1990). He has also described this as the 'background consensus that lies behind all narrative exchange' (quoted in Fischer, 2003: 1999). One issue within development intervention is that such a background consensus is often likely not to exist *a priori* between the different stakeholders, and therefore communicative action cannot establish itself successfully. The issue then becomes whether (or not) a common background consensus can be generated. Chapter 3 explores one attempt to meet this challenge through first exposing different assumptions among stakeholders in a small project that involved many actors in its design.

The second issue concerns cases where a background consensus might be said to exist between stakeholders (for example, because they are all professional engineers). Do not the common assumptions that form the background consensus then limit the possibilities for emancipatory/transformative learning as the participants are trapped within a shared lifeworld whose existence appears, to them, natural and therefore not open to challenge? We explore this issue further in Chapter 4.

The two issues represent a tension for this book, between commonality and difference. Commonality between individuals and groups enables a background consensus that in turn allows for communicative exchange as a basis for shared learning. In addition, commonality provides a secure base for joint organization and action, with potential for learning and innovation.[4] In contrast, under conditions of difference, a background consensus and joint organization and action are more difficult. It is difference, not commonality, however, that is ultimately the source of learning and new knowledge, as we explore further in the section below on theories of learning.

How we promote learning cannot be divorced from our third concern, that of purpose. As pointed out above, purpose parallels the sense of development as a vision of the desirable society. Habermas himself certainly has a vision – that of political emancipation and social justice to be achieved through communicative action. More broadly still, he seeks to contribute towards what he terms the unfinished project of modernity, where reason prevails (Edgar, 2006: 96–100). In this he contrasts with the conventional development studies vision of modernity as a desired state that is achieved, not through communicative action and the learning that emanates from such action, but through a process of 'modernization' where the means become ends. Thus, an early exponent of modernization in the context of development wrote that it comprises the following processes:

> Change from simple and traditionalized techniques towards the application of scientific knowledge.
>
> Evolution from subsistence farming towards commercial production of agricultural goods . . . .
>
> Transition from the use of human and animal power towards industrialization proper . . . .
>
> Movement from farm and village towards urban centres.
>
> (Smelser, 1968: 126)

In so far as this process might be speeded up, technical learning of 'how to do it' is required and it is in this context that the notion of technical assistance (see above) – heralded by the United Nations at its inauguration at the end of the Second World War – was born (Wilson, 2007).

Modernization is not the only development vision, however, and different visions compete with one another. The vision of *empowerment*, for example, favours Habermas's themes of polit-

---

Empowerment

'A desired process by which individuals, typically including the "poorest of the poor", are to take direct control over their lives. Once "empowered" to do so, poor people will then (hopefully) be able to be the agents of their own development' (Thomas, 2000: 35).

ical emancipation and social justice. We choose empowerment as an alternative example of development vision (there are several others) because of its particular association with participatory approaches that espouse, at least implicitly, communicative action.

There is, however, a continuum of senses in which the term 'empowerment' is used. They can be framed by:

- Knowing how to do things for oneself, which is encapsulated in the well-known saying that if you *give* somebody a fish you feed her/him for a day; if you teach her/him *how* to fish you feed her/him for life. This is the sense associated originally with Schumacher's famous book *Small Is Beautiful* (1974). In recent times it has been invoked in terms of providing people with the knowledge that enables them to come on board, and benefit from, capitalist development. It is a vision which, in the Habermasian sense, requires technical knowledge. In principle, it does not require learning through participatory approaches, although these are often justified on effectiveness grounds as the knowledge acquisition needs to be adapted to local context, knowledge of which resides in the recipients.

- Knowing the root causes of one's disempowerment, and knowing collectively how to challenge them. This is the sense most famously associated with radical Brazilian educationalist Paulo Freire and his book, *The Pedagogy of the Oppressed* (1972). It requires both hermeneutic and emancipatory knowledge, and hence a learning process based on open discussion and debate, for which a participatory approach is by definition essential. It comes closest, therefore, to the idea of communicative action.

Chapter 3 explicitly explores participatory and other 'spaces' where these learning processes occur. There, and also in chapters 4 and 6, we also consider further the kinds of knowledge that might be produced, and the extent to which communicative action is possible between participants in these 'action learning spaces'.

Key to our discussion is power, and the relations of power between participants.

Power and knowledge: learning framed by the 'truth'
At its basic level we can say that a relationship of power is evident when *people act in ways which they would otherwise not have chosen.* Often they may be aware of its presence in the form of rules, instructions or threats. It can be at its strongest, however, when people are unaware of its presence – they carry out actions because *they believe* they are the correct things to do or they seem *natural* or *normal* – an effect we discuss below (Kelly and Wilson, 2002).

In development, it is usual to think of *power relations* between people or between social groups (for a summary, see Johnson and Mayoux, 1998: 148–54). At the heart of gender relations, for example, are power relations between men and women. Other examples of power relations include those based on *class* (those who own capital and those who work for it), *religion* (sometimes manifest in relations between leaders and followers), *age* (between young and old) and *ethnicity* (between different ethnic groups).

As for power itself, it is useful to distinguish between three possibilities (see Rowlands, 1997):

1 *Power over*, which is about control over other people through, for example, direct political control or control over resources. *Power over* does not necessarily have to be overt, as when people internalize as 'natural' their power relations with others.

2 *Power to*, which is about having the capacities and capabilities to make choices and engage in actions; in other words the ability to change the conditions of one's existence. It often embodies resistance to *power over.*

3 *Power with*, which is the ability to achieve control through joint action with others.

This book is most concerned with the last two of these – 'power to and with', which we see as being enabled through learning – while being aware of the relevance of 'power over'. Both 'power to' and 'power with' relate strongly to the purpose of learning – to gain capacities and capabilities for development both individually and collectively. 'Power with' also resonates with the idea of promoting learning through collective 'communicative action'.

The work of Foucault focuses on power relations and knowledge, which is why we draw on it here. In Foucault's writings, there are two themes that are particularly relevant to this book: first, the theme of 'governmentality', or the art of modern government (Foucault, 1979), and second the theme of generalized 'regimes of truth' in a society (Foucault, 1980a), which we will explain below. Both themes are linked to Foucault's work on knowledge and power. They are also linked to each other, although it is helpful to take each in turn.

Governmentality. For Foucault the art of modern government requires knowing one's population – its needs and characteristics – in order to make it governable. Government has to learn, therefore, about its population. Quantitatively this can be achieved through statistical gathering, classifying and mapping. Interviews and focus groups can be seen as adding a qualitative dimension.

Foucault's argument poses a challenge. 'Learning for development' seems to have a benign ring. However, different people learn different things for different purposes. We can take an example from the view that participation is the best way to promote development that benefits the poor and excluded. A cynical view, however, might be that, whatever they espouse, development professionals are using it for the purpose of finding out about the 'beneficiaries' and their context in order to do more effectively what they have already decided they intend to do (Wilson, 2006). There is no real intention for it to be an exercise in communicative action (which might question what development professionals do).

The production of 'truth'. This is the process by which a general 'truth' is established in society which then frames what is permissible knowledge, and hence what is learned, in a defined domain. In terms of this book, one might identify a dominant set of macro 'truths' about how to sustain development which then frames interventions at all levels. Examples of dominant contemporary development 'truths' include: market competition drives development; good governance, including democratic representation, is essential; so too are industrialization and globalization (and they are inevitable); alternatively, it is inevitable that many people are left out of development.

Such generalized 'truths' then illuminate the paths one should take in development intervention. For example, when development policy debates become polarized, as they often are, the concept of 'there is no other way' is invoked. An obvious illustration would be the development of a large dam in a country, the construction of which would cause inevitable and significant disruption in its catchment area. There is debate, argument and protest, but the dam proponents will in the end claim that 'there is no other way' in which the drinking water, irrigation and hydro-electric power needs of the country can be met. The intention of such a general truth is to exclude alternative knowledges that might lead to radically different policies.

Foucault researched and wrote extensive and detailed accounts of how 'regimes of truth' are established over time through a multiplicity of relations at and between scales – individuals, collectivities, institutions, the state and so on – that can be defined by (often shifting) relations of power (Foucault, 1980a). For example, his book *Discipline and Punish* (1991) traces the development of a 'truth' about treatment of criminals, from one of administering physical and public violence in the eighteenth century (torture, flogging, public hangings) to disciplining them and reforming them in the privacy of prisons in the nineteenth century.

For Foucault, regimes of truth are maintained by modern apparatuses of government for governmentality purposes – hence the link with the first question. Such apparatuses include learning, by the government and its officials, but also by the population itself learning the 'truth' that is internalized or, to quote Foucault again (1980b), 'normalized' in their daily lives. Again, a further critique of participatory approaches to development is that their underlying purpose is to enable 'beneficiaries' to discover for themselves the 'truths' of liberal capitalist development. Two particular features of regimes of truth (which also apply to the governmentality question), however, are important for this book (Foucault, 1980a).

First, such regimes are not simply constructed by those in 'authority' and then imposed on the social body and the individuals in it. As noted, they arise through a complex negotiation over time. Although they may be rooted in power differences, these differences will have many nuances (for example, men and women in families and households may have different sources of power). Thus regimes of truth cannot simply be described as 'authority' exerting power over those without formal authority. The truth that is constructed from these more subtle dynamics is best described as an accommodation, or acceptance, that permeates society, and is normalized by all, as 'the truth'.

Second, regimes of truth don't actually succeed in disciplining the social body into total acquiescence. These regimes are dynamic entities, forever being challenged, reformed, redefined and (as in the movement from torture of criminals to reforming them) transcended, sometimes over relatively short historical periods. Such changes can be seen as a form of societal learning, although one can never guarantee 100 per cent accommodation or acceptance (for example, the different views about capital punishment in the UK or other countries today).

Foucault is often cited in critical writings on development with reference to overarching 'dominant discourses of development' which frame knowledge about development. 'Discourse' for our purposes can be thought of as the particular ways that truths and regimes of truth are articulated. An example would be the discourse that sees capitalism and globalization as inevitable processes, which in turn leads development interventions to be framed as either ameliorating their unwanted effects (for example, ameliorating poverty and inequality in a society because they can be the source of political instability), and/or ensuring that hitherto excluded people are brought on board to experience the benefits of capitalism and globalization.

Such discourses can act as truths to frame development intervention as described. However, they are also sites of contestation or challenge, and it is the latter that primarily interests us. Thus, synthesizing Foucault and Habermas, the negotiation of truth in development can be seen as a learning process, especially if it is supported by social engagement that approximates to communicative action and that promotes interactions between the technical, hermeneutic and emancipatory domains.

As indicated from the outset, these two sections focusing on Habermas and Foucault have dealt with some of the big ideas which have influenced our approach to this book. As big ideas they tend to deal with knowledge and learning at a macro-scale. If we wish to examine the possibilities for emancipatory learning for development through communicative action, however, we need to explore more what happens in the actual engagements themselves. Such micro-level analysis is the subject not only of our case study chapters, but also of the ideas and theories about everyday learning in practice to which we now turn.

Theories of learning

As we noted in Chapter 1, this book is a critical examination of the kinds of everyday learning that take place between actors engaged in development. Thus even our Chapter 5, which is based on a study of education – or formal learning – for development, focuses on the interaction between formal education and development practice.

For this reason we are interested in the context in which learning occurs and in learning as a social process. Both aspects are particularly important with respect to development. First, an understanding of context is fundamental for engaging with the diversities of history, culture, social relations of power and of everyday life, as well as with wider national and global settings. Second, development involves the engagement of many actors in continuous learning, innovation and change, in particular to address and transform relations of poverty, inequality and subordination.

With these caveats, it is still useful to examine theories of learning that have arisen from the field of education and educational philosophy as they can inform – and some of them address – learning as a social process. They are, in effect, social theories of learning. It is particularly useful to refer to those writers who have studied the relationship between learning and work, and between learning and action.

For example, Hager has counterposed two views of learning that illustrate why a conventional educational view may not be appropriate to the dynamic social setting of work, although both are based on human reflective capacity. The first (conventional view) is that learning involves accumulating ideas, reflecting on or thinking about them, and being able to retrieve them (a bit like the learning that is generally tested for in education systems); the second, more appropriate to analysing learning at work, sees learning as contextual, multi-skilled and involving tacit as well as formal processes of reflection – it changes learners and it changes the world on which they act: learning is 'action in the world' (Hager, 2004: 246). The second view is a social – contextual – theory of learning which challenges the 'learning as acquisition' idea of the first.

The second idea of learning is linked to ideas of 'social constructivism'[5] in which knowledge is seen as an outcome of ways of being, relations, behaviours and practices in groups, which are, again, contextually influenced – whether in a workplace or a particular social and cultural setting. Social constructivist views of learning were theorized by the famous educationalist John Dewey, amongst others, who developed ideas about experiential learning which have since been used and built on by many writers and researchers. Of particular interest in this book are the ideas of David Kolb (1984), who further modelled experiential learning as a constant and iterative process that involves grasping, reflecting on and conceptualizing concrete experience leading to new knowledge and action on the world.[6]

While this view seems very attractive in relation to development, particularly given its close links with action, constructivist views also have their critics. In relation to the links between learning and work, Young suggests that such approaches are partial. He distinguishes interest-based and process-based constructivism: the first assumes that any knowledge is based on social interests and reflects power relations, while the second is concerned with knowledge as contextual or situated (2004: 193). Both aspects are of concern to us in this book. Young's critique is that the main, or only, issue for the interest approach is who has power, while process-based approaches are not contextually specific enough. With respect to the latter, Young notes that 'many jobs . . . require knowledge involving theoretical ideas shared by a community of specialists that are not tied to specific contexts; such knowledge enables those who have acquired it to move beyond specific situations' (*ibid.*: 193–4). This particular issue is something that we challenge in Chapter 4 in our discussion of North–South learning in practitioner-to-practitioner partnerships, where it seems that even communities of specialists have contextualized knowledge.

Young, however, does make an interesting addition to this discussion, one relevant to learning for development. He suggests that 'social realist' approaches can provide an additional dimension to our understandings of learning and knowledge production: 'although all knowledge is historical and social in origins, it is its particular social origins that give it its objectivity, and it is this that enables knowledge to transcend the conditions of its production' (*ibid.*: 194). Thus, for Young, identifying those conditions is crucial – which of course links back to both social interests (power) and context. However the prospect of transcending those conditions is also attractive to learning for development, as it suggests, in a parallel argument to that of Habermas, the possibility of transformation.

Transformation is an imprecise concept in the social sciences. It tends to be used to encapsulate thinking and action that reframe and recast current practices, whether embedded in institutions (or the institutions themselves) or within organizations and other social groupings. Hickey and Mohan suggest that, to be effective, social transformation has to go beyond the local and be 'linked to a radical development project' (2004: 15). By the latter is meant a wider process of change, not a 'project' in the development intervention sense of the word. However, other writers have used the concept of transformation in a much more bounded sense: for example, Fowler has used it to denote 'major reappraisal and organisational reorientation, but not necessarily a shift in purpose or mission' (2000: 156). Transformation may be an idealized view of what is likely to happen in practice. Moreover, transformation may not be apparent until a period of time has elapsed and other events and processes have taken place. However, it is useful to have a concept that encapsulates the general idea of, and potential for, reframing, rethinking and recasting approaches to particular aspects of social life.

The dialogue between conceptualizing learning and work, and learning and action, can be taken further in terms of its relevance for development and the idea of transformation. There have been many attempts to categorize types of learning, which have also been contested and criticized (Coffield *et al.*, 2004). One well-known typology is that of Entwistle (1997) who suggested that there are three main ways in which learners approach learning: a surface approach, in which knowledge is simply reproduced by the learner; a strategic approach, in which learners target their efforts to particular kinds of achievement; and a deep approach, which focuses on a critical understanding of meanings and relationships. The deep approach is also said to be transformative. The surface and strategic approaches seem to parallel Habermas's technical domain of knowledge, the deep approach the hermeneutic and emancipatory domains.

Such categories should not be used in a simplistic way, however – typically, learners may use more than one approach to learning, depending on the situation and the desired outcomes, as we find when we investigate the relationship between formal learning and changes in development practice (Chapter 5). Nevertheless one can use such categories in broad terms to reflect on what kind of learning seems to be taking place in development action. As we note in Chapter 4, some types of practitioner-to-practitioner learning reproduce inappropriate models from the North that are assumed to have universal qualities in the South. On the other hand, challenges arising from shared experiences can also transform behaviours in both North and South.

The Kolbean model of experiential learning is also concerned with transformation, both when the learner reflects on experience and when the learner takes new action (or experiments). We have suggested that this is the basis of an 'action learning space', a concept we return to in the final section of this chapter.

Our concern in this book is with collective as well as individual action, whether that collectivity is within an organization or a community group, between professional peers or many stakeholders working in development. So how does joint learning come about? As noted by Hodkinson and Hodkinson (2004) in relation to learning and work, there are several theories that have been used to explain learning in work groups. Hodkinson and Hodkinson analyse three types of learning: that already known to others, the further development of existing capabilities, and learning that is new to everyone. (It can probably be seen that these are rather similar to Entwistle's categories.) In each case, learning may be planned or unintentional. The first type of learning – similar to Entwistle's category of learning as reproduction – can result in bringing someone (or a group of people) into an existing 'community of practice'. A community of practice is a concept used by Wenger (1998) to denote a group (or 'community', in a metaphorical sense) of people who share a common purpose or passion, engage in joint discussions and activities, and build up or share a common repertoire of skills and practices. The idea emerged from a study of apprenticeship carried out by Lave and Wenger (1991), which argued that learning is situated and embedded in social settings. Thus apprentices may start on the margins of a group which embodies considerable expertise and, through learning in the group over time, become equally expert and central to the practice and reproduction of its activities. The concept of communities of practice is increasingly used by international development organizations and writers about development to describe fora for building shared knowledge and approaches. An issue for such socially embedded learning, though, is the extent to which current knowledge (or 'truths' in Foucauldian terms) is reflected on or contested in ways that lead to new knowledge.

The second type of learning noted by Hodkinson and Hodkinson – the further development of existing capabilities (somewhat similar to Entwistle's strategic approach to learning) – can be aligned to capacity-building approaches to development, while the third type – learning which is new to everyone – could in principle be akin to transformation. While transformation from a learning perspective may mean a fundamental change in ideas, in an action sense it may mean a change in social relations – for example, a change in relations of power. In the Kolbean perspective, learning and action are intimately linked, as they are for Habermas's emancipatory knowledge domain (although Habermas does not explicitly refer to learning). The reality is often more challenging, however, as we shall see in the case studies in this book.

The concept of communities of practice has been suggested as one mechanism through which joint learning can take place, whether to bring people into an existing set of practices – which can thus be a force as much *against* as *for* change – or to further the development of capabilities, probably along incremental lines. Communities of practice appear to have commonalities with the Habermasian notion of a shared lifeworld.[7] They are generally conceived as informal rather than formal or institutional processes, although attempts to construct or promote communities of practice in recent times (rather than seeing them as emergent from particular situations) have given a rather more formal presence to them. There is however considerable debate about whether communities of practice can simply be constructed, given that they fundamentally rely on trust between participants which is built up over time.

Thus although emergent (and possibly constructed) communities of practice may give rise to learning in an organizational sense, they cannot be equated with organizational learning *per se*. Organizational learning has in turn been theorized, notably by Argyris and Schön, as a social dynamic in which the 'mismatch between expected and actual results of action' (1996: 16) provides feedback loops which can lead to changes in behaviour – characterized as single-loop learning (more but better action) and double-loop learning (different action). Such learning may occur at the individual level but would have to be embedded in the routines of the organization to have a wider impact.

In their approach to organizational learning Argyris and Schön raise a more general point about how learning occurs – one that is particularly significant for development and constitutes a further 'big idea' for this book, thus far considered only briefly in our discussion of Habermas. Many writers have pointed out how 'difference' is a key aspect of learning: that is, that we learn from difference, not from things that are the same as those we already (think we) know or believe to be the case. In other words, it is through contestation and different experiences and different knowledges that we learn. This has been a feature of writing on 'conversational learning': 'a process whereby learners construct meaning and transform experiences into knowledge through conversations' (Kolb *et al.*, 2002: 51). Based on experiential learning, conversational learning takes place 'through interplay of opposites and contradictions' (*ibid.*: 53). As noted by these writers, 'learning is the process of making the strange familiar' (Baker *et al.*, 2002: 2). This cornerstone of learning is crucial for learning in, through and for development action, in which there may be many differences of perspective, culture and vision, as well as everyday processes and practices. We will see incidences of such difference and actors learning from difference (as well as the obstacles to learning from difference) in the chapters that follow.

A final issue for this section is the relationship between individual and wider learning within or between organizations, wider groupings of people and stakeholders in development. As will be seen from case studies in this book, individual learning for development does not necessarily bring about organizational or institutionalized change. Yet trying to build knowledge and wider learning communities is a key concern of many international development organizations and has given rise to mechanisms for sharing knowledge and information with the expectation of greater and more generalized learning. One particular and increasingly common mechanism is through online platforms, whether used for the micro-level purposes we describe in Chapter 6 or for worldwide discussion fora. While electronic media have the potential to democratize information and make it accessible to millions of people (the digital divide notwithstanding), online information and communication processes are subject to the same issues that we have raised above in relation to learning and knowledge: whose information, whose interests, and what are the contexts and kinds of processes that are involved? As many writers have noted, for online conferences and discussion fora to be successful learning platforms, trust is also paramount (Barab *et al.*, 2003; Schwen and Hara, 2003).

Overall, there are some fundamental propositions from this discussion that inform the content and analysis of the book. The first is that learning is situated in social settings, which in turn inform the nature and content of learning. The second is that learning is based on the interaction of experience – the basis of tacit knowledge, or the bulk of the iceberg under the water, as Stiglitz (1999) has noted – and other forms of learning through interactions with others as well as interactions with texts (codified knowledge). In particular, learning comes about through interaction with different knowledges, experiences and ways of being and doing, and is a cornerstone of development action. The third proposition is that learning is influenced by social relations, which include those of power as well as those that contest power. The final proposition is that the relationship between individual learning and organizational and institutionalized learning is a complex phenomenon both to explain and to achieve in practice (as our case studies will testify).

Action learning spaces

In the preceding sections we have considered learning as a process into which all human beings are drawn through our ability to reflect and communicate with one another. We considered learning in relation to knowledge and power and the constraints imposed by dominant truths, as well as the possibility of transcending them. In the last section, we further examined learning as mediated by social relations and settings at the micro level. We have not yet, however, conceptualized where and when learning might occur.

We have suggested elsewhere (Johnson and Wilson, 2009) and reiterate here that the concept of 'action learning space' can help identify those moments or dynamics through which learning has the potential to occur, or, as we said in Chapter 1, create 'opportunities for learning through the process of social engagement and joint action, and the interaction of codified and tacit knowledge in everyday practice'. Action learning derives from the Kolbean view of experiential learning outlined above, while 'space' is that moment of social interaction which triggers new knowledge, understanding and insights as well as new practices, tools, techniques and skills. Such interaction may be framed by, for example:

- a joint project or problem that needs solving;
- a shared engagement in some aspect of social life.

The idea of action learning space allows for the many cross-cutting interactions, events, histories and experiences that influence learning and knowledge production. Overall, such spaces are about building shared understanding through shared experience, which in turn leads to the potential for communicative action for new knowledge and practice.

Although trust is a key ingredient of shared learning, action learning spaces are not necessarily safe – indeed they may be conflictive. While the rules and norms that define social interaction may create the possibility of learning, learning can also challenge the safeness of the relationship and even the rules and norms – the shared lifeworld – in which is it based. Understanding the nature of these spaces and their social relations thus helps to make visible the sometimes uncomfortable processes that are involved.

Finally, we should note the analytical and normative dimensions of this concept. We have used the concept of action learning space as though it is a process that can be created intentionally. While this may be true in some circumstances, such spaces are also very likely to be self-generating, or to be an outcome of other processes. Thus development actors may aim to create the conditions for such learning but there may be many ways in which action learning occurs (or, for that matter, is blocked). We shall find examples of both kinds of process in subsequent chapters.

Notes

1 See <http://dgroups.org/>.

2 In dictionary terms, to learn is 'to get knowledge of . . . or skill in . . . by study, experience or teaching' (*Shorter Oxford English Dictionary*, 1965).

3 Unless indicated otherwise, this section draws on original texts by Habermas. We are, however, indebted to the pointers provided by Andrew Edgar's *Habermas: the Key Concepts* (2006).

4 This point has been made by Velasco, 2009.

5 Social constructivism is closely associated with social constructionism. Both are concerned with how knowledge and learning are developed in social contexts. Social constructivism, used by educationalists and psychologists, generally refers to the individual learning that takes place in, and is influenced by, a social context, such as within a group. Thus groups create collective knowledge and meaning. Social constructionism is more sociological and tends to refer to how individuals and groups create and give meaning to their own realities through their interactions with each other and in the world. Both dimensions are part of the processes that we have analysed in this book.

6 Kolb's own definition of learning is a little different from the *Shorter Oxford English Dictionary*: 'the process whereby knowledge is created through the transformation of experience' (1984: 38).

7 In an interesting study, Lave and Wenger (1991) showed how apprentices were brought into the shared lifeworld (although they did not use this term) of their trade through what they termed 'legitimate peripheral participation'.

3 | Contestation and Learning between Multiple Stakeholders

One of the biggest challenges for development action – wherever in the world – is how to work with stakeholders who have different social histories, interests, identities and values. Partnership, participation, inclusion and empowerment are all embedded in contemporary development discourse and it is assumed that buy-in from stakeholders is essential (if not sufficient) to give interventions a chance of success. However, as anyone who has ever been part of a partnership or a participant in a forum with many stakeholders will know, working with other individuals and organizations can be extremely challenging, and involves a lot of learning. Why is it so challenging, what kind of learning is required, and how does it come about? These are questions that this chapter seeks to answer. In addition the chapter will examine the role of contestation in learning and how mediation or facilitation in such contexts can provide an important function.

Working with many stakeholders is an intrinsic aspect of development action in that social change involves a range of organizations and skills to bring it about. For example, it is not possible to design and implement a policy for structural reform or even a small micro-finance project without taking into account the activities of and impacts on the different actors who might be implicated. It is of course possible to model a design and carry it out without consulting different actors. Many forms of sophisticated modelling that inform economic policy do not involve the conscious inputs of actors, even though such modelling may be based on data about those actors that have been gathered in other ways. Such models may have success but they may also contain assumptions that lead to unexpected or negative consequences, as was the experience of structural adjustment programmes which aimed to liberalize economies and reduce the role of the state in the 1980s and 1990s. Although lack of consultation with or involvement of other actors do not in themselves lead to failure, we shall see in Chapter 4 that even computer models can be improved by consulting with those who are likely to implement or are expected to benefit from the intervention. This is because there are many human elements and contextual factors that are difficult to take into account. Modellers need to *learn* about them and learn from them.

Development interventions are highly political acts. They involve choices over resources – their generation, distribution and use. They are also political because, in principle, they seek to address poverty, inequality and social injustice. Such deliberate attempts to do so are likely to challenge existing orders (or to lead to challenges, whether intended or unintended), no matter in how small a way.

The purposes of development, and the unintended or negative effects of many development interventions, have thus fuelled the call for participation and partnership, as we have seen. It is assumed that participation and partnership result in better development – that inclusion of actors and working in partnership provide buy-in and access to different knowledges, thereby leading to more appropriate interventions. Participation and partnership are also linked to rights-based development and to giving people a voice.

A key question is whether and how different actors are included in determining and carrying out (as well as benefiting from) intervention, and whether and how their different knowledges and human and physical resources lead to new and innovative policies and actions that could not be achieved by a single actor alone. However, bringing together groups and organizations with different social positions and purposes is challenging. For example, the position of a savings-and-loan or micro-credit organization, which works to serve the developmental goals of its members, is very different from that of an international NGO providing funds or training for such an organization, or a research institute promoting new production technologies for the members. The different social and organizational positions, and the different histories, interests, identities and values they represent, present a complex dynamic. Moreover, groups and organizations are not necessarily homogeneous within themselves. Such considerations mean that joint action requires learning about and between actors, and may require negotiation or mediation processes.

This chapter examines some of these issues through the experience of a small action research project in a multi-actor domain, carried out by the authors in Zimbabwe in 1999. It argues that mediating contestation over social goals arising from the different perspectives and knowledges of actors can be the basis for a learning partnership (even if informally constituted). The chapter will first examine some ideas about inter-organizational dynamics, the challenges for participation in a socially differentiated world, and how the idea of action learning spaces may be applied in this context – including, in this instance, an action learning tool used by the authors. It will then look at the attempt to create space for action learning in the case of a development and environment intervention in Zimbabwe. Finally, the chapter will reflect on these dynamics and the potential of facilitated, structured settings in learning for development.

Some concepts

In this section we look at some key conceptual elements of learning between multiple stakeholders: the nature of inter-organizational relationships; the participation debate, particularly with respect to social differentiation; and process issues involved in action learning spaces.

Inter-organizational relationships
The theme of inter-organizational relationships has been perti-

nent to development managers, who face the constant challenge of how to work with a number of organizations in carrying out interventions. Here we briefly consider the work of Robinson *et al.* (2000) who use a heuristic device to examine inter-organizational relationships by distinguishing types of relationship: those of competition, coordination and cooperation.[1] While these are ideal types and the authors make it clear that they coexist and overlap in reality, they provide a heuristic handle for analysing inter-organizational dynamics in development action, whether in interventions by the state, by multilateral, bilateral or non-governmental organizations, or through the activities and roles of the private sector. One driver for paying attention to these relationships is the growing emphasis on partnership, as we have mentioned. As noted above, working in partnership raises considerable challenges, not least in managing the unequal power relations between groups and organizations, and taking cognizance of the wider institutional context of public action and policy development.

Development action in inter-organizational domains is thus dependent on learning processes. Examples might include mapping relationships to learn about the influence and significance of different actors, and to understand thought processes and differences. Other learning processes are examining assumptions, asking questions and reframing ideas and proposals. Yet all of these are hard to engage in without a degree of trust between actors. Trust may have to be built. For example, Vangen and Huxham (2003) have analysed cyclical trust-building loops where positive experiences of working together are self-reinforcing. Intermediaries may also be needed: brokers, mediators and facilitators to support a mutual learning and trust-building process, as well as to make interests, values and desired goals explicit. Hewitt and Robinson (2000: 316) mention Inskip's (1994) concept of 'network agents': 'middle-level organizations that connect policy and services planning and development by facilitating communications between the macro (government generally) and micro (community groups or individuals) levels of governance'. Such agents can provide a mechanism for mutual learning.

Social differentiation and power relations can affect the outcome of any type of inter-organizational dynamic, even in partnerships based on cooperation. Harriss notes instances where 'the language of partnership thinly veils power differences' (2000: 227). However he also underlines the importance of trust in enabling cooperation, particularly of the self-organizing kind, where groups and organizations are able to build trust incrementally through a learning process. We will see some embryonic elements of this dynamic in our case study below, in which difference and contestation can also force actors in self-organizing partnerships to question their assumptions and to reframe the basis of their cooperation. An important question is how to enable this process to happen in such a way that contestation is a constructive source of ideas and innovation rather than a process that drives people apart.

Participation
As we have seen (see box on page 15), the huge growth in interest in participation represents an attempt by academics and practitioners to address the challenge of including previously excluded people in determining, designing and benefiting from development interventions. From participation's early proponents, such as Robert Chambers, to the more recent critics of participation and participatory approaches, there has been an ongoing concern to provide a 'voice' for poor and disenfranchised populations in development. A large literature has sprung up to conceptualize or to critique participation; and either to promote participatory forms of investigation for policy development or to criticize them in terms of how they are carried out in practice. In the broadest of terms, this critique (1) sees participation as a form of co-option to a development process whose agendas are directed by governments and institutions in the North; (2) accuses participation of conceptually valorizing local over wider processes of change;

(3) on the practical front, finds participatory techniques to be superficially conceptualized and implemented, not properly taking power relations into account – nor considering that they might even be reinforced by such interventions.

The result of this debate has been to attempt to reframe participation in new ways, succinctly brought together in Hickey and Mohan (2004). Some key ideas stand out. One, mentioned earlier, is the proposal to recast participation as active and radical citizenship: 'a broader range of socio-political practices, or expressions of agency, through which people extend their status and rights as members of particular political communities, thereby increasing their control over socio-economic resources' (Mohan and Hickey, 2004: 66). Another is to clarify the conditions of participation. Cornwall suggests that there are two kinds of participatory 'space': 'popular' and 'invited'. Popular spaces are 'those arenas in which people join together, often with others like them, in collective action, self-help initiatives or everyday sociality', while invited spaces are 'constructed opportunities for "the people", or their representatives, to come together with those who represent public authorities' or 'more complex multi-stakeholder institutions involving representatives from civil society, the private sector, government, donors and lenders' (2004: 76).

Although there may be instances in which Cornwall's two types of space might not be clearly distinct (for example, collective action is often initiated or championed by a particular group or organization that might invite others to join; the Environmental Action Group in our case study below is such an example), we are mainly concerned with invited spaces in this chapter. We will see that the potential for learning in such spaces is strongly influenced by power relations and by how difference and commonality are understood and acted on. Cornwall notes that invited spaces for participation may strongly reflect wider power relations and the social position of different participants. However, bringing different actors together also has its own dynamic and may give rise to new forms of contestation and resistance. As a result, 'spaces created with one purpose in mind may be used by those who engage in them for something quite different' (*ibid.*: 80–1). Through such processes, it is possible (but not necessary) that learning for development occurs. But much depends on how the dynamics are worked through by participants: as Cornwall notes, 'what counts as knowledge . . . requires more than simply seeking to allow everyone to speak and asserting the need to listen' (*ibid.*: 84).

Action on and working through contestation and conflict as a learning process present further challenges. For example, Leeuwis (2000) argues that participatory approaches to development rely fundamentally on two processes: (1) social learning for planning and decision making, which are in turn based on (2) Habermas's (1990) idea of 'communicative action'. Leeuwis argues that this conceptual underpinning of participation is one of the reasons why it runs into difficulties. As we have noted above, actors come to participation with different social histories, interests and values; they probably also have different aims and goals. Leeuwis thus suggests that participants are more likely to engage in *strategic*[2] rather than communicative action in order to achieve their own ends. He gives several examples that support this claim and suggests that, given that conflict is nearly always present in participatory processes, basing participation on the assumption that increased knowledge and understanding will necessarily change actors' courses of action is misguided. Instead, Leeuwis suggests that negotiation and negotiators are required to create the preconditions and institutions for social learning and cooperation (Leeuwis, 2000: 947).

Action learning spaces, social difference and communities of practice

So what are the implications of this discussion for learning between multiple stakeholders for development? Is it possible to do what Leeuwis suggests? Earlier, we introduced the concepts of action learning spaces and communities of practice. We return to them briefly again here, and also outline a framework for an agenda-setting process (for mutual learning) that the authors developed and used to investigate multi-stakeholder activity in Zimbabwe.

We have said that action learning spaces are spaces in which people with different histories, relations and world views are able to come together, learn through expression and acknowledgement of difference, and engage in new approaches to development, however modest those new approaches might be. Leeuwis is sceptical that such processes can occur without a negotiation function. Yet there are other dimensions which can both promote – as well as hinder – learning and action. For example, we have made the argument that communities of practice – groups of people with a shared enterprise, mutual engagement in that enterprise, and a shared repertoire of knowledge and skills (Wenger, 1998) – can both limit and promote new learning. On one hand, communities of practice have a tendency to institutionalize ('reify') existing knowledge, making it difficult to challenge it; on the other hand, groups of people from different communities of practice (involving different knowledges and social identities based on their different practices) have the potential to learn from each other. Often it's the jolt of contestation or conflict that can lead either to entrenched positions or, by contrast, to reframing the issues. Learning for development is thus a site of struggle – like all social change – and often requires some structured processes to enable dialogue that leads to accommodation and change (Isaacs, 1993).

In the late 1990s, the authors of this book developed a framework for joint agenda setting, which is a process of negotiation that arises from stakeholders learning about each other. The framework consisted of examining core *assumptions* about the problem to be addressed and what needed to be done; acknowledging the need for *accountability* in agreed actions to be undertaken – both in the sense of responsibility and in being able to provide an account of the action taken; and developing shared understandings of what actions and processes had led to what outcomes and why – a sense of *attribution*. We thus called this framework the '3 As' (assumptions, accountability and attribution) and proposed it as a learning and negotiating tool for interventions in which there are many stakeholders. We now go on to examine how it was used to investigate and promote learning in such an initiative in Zimbabwe.

Creating space for action learning and inclusive agenda setting

The following case study is based on research carried out in Zimbabwe in 1998. The concerns behind this study mirrored those in this chapter: how is it possible to include all stakeholders – especially hitherto excluded groups – in the definition, design and implementation of interventions? What kinds of learning processes are needed and how can they be sustained? The project we investigated was an initiative to bring together development and environment concerns by focusing on the problem of solid waste management (SWM) and income generation for poor people by setting up a recycling project in a mining town to the north of the capital, Harare. Our link to this initiative was through a Zimbabwean national NGO whose members of staff had studied the MSc in Development Management at the Open University. The NGO had been promoting Environmental Action Groups (EAGs) in Zimbabwe and this was a project of the EAG in the mining town. The EAG included members of the private sector (mines and local retail), public sector (local offices of different ministries and the environmental health department of the local authority), and members of voluntary groups working in poor communities in the town. One of the latter, a church-based group, had been approached for assistance by a group of widows of AIDS victims, who had formed an association. It was subsequently suggested that the widows' association could both help contribute to solving the problem of SWM in the town and also gain an income through a recycling scheme. In what follows, we briefly outline the challenges of SWM and the thinking behind the scheme. We describe the research process that took place, and show how contestation between groups and interests became a source of learning for those involved in this initiative. In doing so, we examine the intersection of different communities of practice and the importance of mediators in providing a structured process of agenda setting for the ongoing negotiation and implementation of the project.

The challenges to resource-strapped local authorities of managing solid waste are considerable. At the time of this project, Zimbabweans were experimenting with private sector franchises, but not with great success. In the mining town, there was unequal distribution of waste collection, primarily targeting the wealthier, tax-paying areas whereas the growing population in the poor settlements around the town were not well serviced. There was a growing waste management problem, in part because of the population increase in 'high density' areas fuelled by rural–urban migration, and in part because of the nature of the mining industry as well as an increase in sugar cane production in local agriculture (both create considerable waste products). However, rather than turning to private franchises, it was suggested that the challenge be managed through a combination of public education and engagement of 'the community' in targeted projects such as the proposed recycling scheme to be carried out by the widows' association.

The EAG's discussions of the project had not, until that point, involved the widows directly. The church group claimed to represent their interests in the EAG: a kind of proxy inclusion. It was also not clear how the project was to be carried out. The first step of our research was to attend an EAG meeting and to propose that potentially we could help members take their initiative forward by (1) interviewing key stakeholders (including the widows) to build a picture of the different perspectives, and (2) holding a workshop with a structured set of activities that would help them clarify what they were going to do and develop an agenda for the next steps. At the same time, the process would allow us to research our 3 As framework as well as the issues being addressed. We tested the workshop design with members of the environmental NGO (and subsequently modified it), and also carried out a debriefing session with the NGO after the workshop, as it was this organization that would have a future mediating function.

We were working with two main hypotheses. The first was that social divisions have to be overtly recognized, negotiated and represented in such interventions, both to build coherence and to ensure the participation of groups who otherwise might be excluded. The second was that action learning can assist the expression of differences (including different knowledges and areas of expertise), as well as commonalities, and thus lead to some form of accommodation.

Action learning requires explicit agendas for negotiation to bridge the divisions and carry out joint action. We also suggested that it requires some form of structured facilitation. In this instance we used the 3 As outlined above to structure a workshop around the following questions (adapted from Johnson and Wilson, 2000, Table 1):

Questions about assumptions
- What is the project expected to achieve?
- What activities will be undertaken by the project?
- What do you need to do in order to set up the project?
- How will the project last?

Questions about accountability
- Which are the organizations involved in this project?
- Do any organizations have to be created?
- What are the jobs or roles of organizations involved in this project?
- Who will make the decisions, and about what?

Questions about attribution

- What things would you like to find out in order to keep track of the project?
- How can you find out about the things you have listed so that everyone involved can learn from the project?
- If you discovered that only half the households were sorting their waste, how would you find out why the others were not doing it?
- If you found out that the incomes of the people doing the recycling had improved, how would you know if it was because of this project or for some other reason?

It will immediately be seen that these questions were intended to elicit responses about the 3 As without asking about them directly. In the workshop, participants were divided into four small groups with facilitators (see box overleaf), with each working through the above questions (with additional prompts and sub-questions) and summarizing their answers and views on flipcharts. At the beginning of the exercise, we presented the findings from the interviews, as well as explaining the purpose and objectives of the day. At the end of the day, we summarized what people had produced during the workshop and created a new agenda of questions that still had to be answered. In putting people into groups, we deliberately had one group (Group 4) that comprised the direct representatives of the widows' association (association members, that is, not proxy representation), and other people known to them, so that they had some level of trust and support. They also worked in their first language, Shona, which enabled them to express themselves freely. The other workshop participants were allocated randomly to groups by giving everyone a number. In spite of this, one group (Group 1) coincidentally contained mainly environment professionals from the private and public sectors. It is in the comparison of the 'widows group' and the 'environment professionals group' that some of the interesting areas of difference and contestation lie.

Composition of the workshop groups and facilitators

Group 1   Environmental health officer from the town council
             Environmental health technician from a local mine
             Environmental health technician, Ministry of
             Health
             Environmental health trainee from the town council
             Home-based care representative
             Facilitator: UK researchers

Group 2   Home-Based Care representative
             Informal traders' association representative
             Church-based group representative
             Environmental health technician from the town
             council
             Facilitator: environmental NGO representative

Group 3   Home-Based Care representative
             Informal traders' association representative
             Education officer, Ministry of Education
             Extension officer, Forestry Commission
             Local NGO representative
             Facilitator: environmental NGO representative

Group 4   Church pastor, member of church-based group
             Minister involved with widows' association and
             Home-Based Care
             Widow
             Widow
             Widow
             Facilitator: environmental NGO representative

Note: Home-Based Care is an HIV/AIDS support organization. This box is adapted from data in Table 2 of Johnson and Wilson, 2000.

We shall examine the key areas of contestation that came through from the interviews and the workshop. An important aspect is that they were not explicitly realized beforehand and were learning points for stakeholders. Where appropriate, we shall identify how views changed between the interviews and the workshop. We then go on to reflect on the nature of participation and the potential emergence of communities of practice.

Different views on problem definition and aims of the project
In the interviews, the town council and Ministry of Health were both concerned by the lack of resources to manage waste, whereas other public sector officials were concerned about the lack of public education and public action on waste management, and to some extent about the impact on the environment (the environmental NGO was one of these concerned parties). All concurred with the need for 'community'[3] involvement. By contrast, the widows' problem definition was 'how to make a living', a view supported to some extent by the church-based group – their concern was to 'help the poor and needy', and they also identified the environment as a challenge. The aims of the project mapped on to these views: there were many specific expressions of the general aim of improving waste management, educating people and changing attitudes, and mobilizing the community. The widows, however, supported in part by the church-based group, saw the aim of the project as contributing to their livelihoods.

During the course of the workshop, the importance of income generation and poverty alleviation grew in many participants' perceptions of the aims of the project. In addition, greater awareness of health hazards was shown, and of the potential for changing attitudes and practices. There was also increasing awareness of some important assumptions: that the project would be economically viable and that the widows' income would improve; that the project would gain support from the residents; and that the community would support the town council in its endeavour to mobilize popular engagement in waste management. The widows, however, demonstrated a much more realistic perspective in terms of the practical viability of the project: would the residents hand over their waste (given that much waste is already recycled in poor households)? Would the council pass a by-law to make sure they did? Would there be help with transport, a recycling site and equipment? These questions were posed embedded in an assumption by the widows that if they were to proceed with this project, these elements would need to be in place. Through the course of the workshop discussions, their interests were being made explicit and became a point of negotiation.

Different views on inter-organizational relationships and participation

As will be apparent from the box on page 56, there were many stakeholders in this initiative, reflecting the diverse membership of the EAG. Their sense of their own roles and how they related to other stakeholders was going to be important for the leadership and management of the project. During the interviews, it became apparent that coordination was the dominant model. There was less agreement on who would be the coordinator, however, and an element of competition between the public sector institutions was evident. It was an environmental health technician from the private sector who suggested that there should be a partnership between the town council and 'the community' – but with the town council as the lead partner.

Pursuing these issues in the workshop through discussion of the accountability questions provided more insights into the inter-organizational dynamics, in particular different ideas about management and control, and the terms of participation of the widows. The town council, the EAG, the church-based group and the widows' association were all put forward as possible candidates for managing the project, although participants found it hard to distinguish strategic and day-to-day management functions, and no participant, including the widows, thought the widows should have exclusive management and control. That this was discussed openly, if not resolved, was an advance on positions taken during the interviews, in which the widows were seen to some extent as simple beneficiaries, needing to be carefully selected in terms of their participation.

Some of these differences – and the pending nature of the issues raised – were also reflected in discussion of the attribution questions. For example, the 'environmental professionals group' (Group 1) still focused mainly on management and accountability concerns, while the focus of the 'widows' group' (Group 4) was how their livelihoods would be sustained, and how they would set up and keep their own rules and norms of conduct. These different perspectives were also reflected in the discussion of the attribution 'what if?' questions. While Group 1 pursued a potential mode of inquiry to find out why residents were (hypothetically) not handing over their waste for recycling, Group 4 was mainly concerned with incentives and sanctions. These issues were thus potential arenas for establishing a collaborative and learning partnership or potential arenas of conflict and pursuit of individual group interests. Realizing these differences in the course of the workshop contributed to the future negotiation agenda.

Participation

The workshop was an example of an 'invited' space for participation, in that it was engineered by the environmental NGO with our inputs. Although the EAG was a forum for members of different sectors of the town to participate in the environmental health and future development of the town from this perspective, it had not included a key actor in its discussions for the recycling scheme. The widows' participation in the scheme was assumed, and was being brokered by the church-based group. By involving the widows in the workshop, and having structured the workshop in a particular way, including providing the widows with their own 'invited' space as a group, the EAG members rapidly learnt that there was a set of issues that had to be negotiated with them – with respect both to the control and management of the project and to the practical dimensions and feasibility of what was being proposed. Yet this space was not simply a question of bringing people together: it was the structured and purposeful process behind the discussions that enabled participants to learn about the areas of contestation and difference. For the widows, an important learning outcome was that they had identified a key stakeholder from their point of view: while previously their role had been mediated by the church-based group, they quickly realized the relative power and authority of the town council – it could (to a certain extent) make things happen. Thus if the 'community' were to engage in public action on waste management, it was clear that the town council had a responsibility to help create the framework for it to happen as well as to provide some of the physical infrastructure. The widows made this an explicit demand. While other actors would indeed help to engage the wider constituency in public education and change in waste disposal practice, for the recycling scheme the key negotiation would be between the council and the widows.

Different 'communities of practice'

Looking at this process from a critical communities of practice perspective, one can see that although there were randomly chosen groups (apart from the widows) in the workshop, the representatives came with identities, knowledges and practices that to some extent were bounded and to some extent were shared – their commonalities and differences. Prior to the workshop, interviews with the stakeholders indicated the worlds of practice that each inhabited. Thus the town council interviewees focused on the role of the council in waste management, its status in the town as a potential coordinator of partnership activity, its technical expertise in waste management, and its need to meet political agendas. By contrast, the church-based group focused on Christian mission, which combined assisting poor people with helping to realize talents in the community. Yet their repertoire of skills was not simply in the faith arena: during the interviews, it became clear that they had thought through the practical dimensions of waste collection and how the recycling scheme could be organized. Likewise, interviewees from the local offices of the ministries of education and health, the Department of Natural Resources and the Forestry Commission, all of which were represented in the EAG, came at the issues from their identities as educators, health workers, et cetera, bringing forward particular areas of expertise and practice – or, in Habermasian terms, their different lifeworlds.

Of course the EAG itself can be characterized as a community of practice in that it had a mutual interest in the environmental health of the town, a shared enterprise in trying to achieve it (and specifically a shared enterprise in the recycling project); it also gathered the different areas of expertise into a repertoire that could be drawn on in addressing waste management in the town, and in trying to address some of the underlying issues such as poverty and exclusion. However, the interviews and workshop highlighted that, in practice, the EAG represented a set of interlocking and overlapping lifeworlds with different identities and boundaries, in which some dimensions and expertises were shared and others not.

We have focused mainly on the environmental professionals and the widows in this chapter, yet a closer examination of the other participants and their organizations (and the inter-organizational relationships) would also have revealed shared and unshared knowledges and practices. A key outcome of the research was the learning that different EAG members gained by focusing in a structured way on a particular problem they had to solve. It could be said that this mediated process was the first step to building communicative action. A future learning outcome to aim for might have been the building of a shared knowledge and skill repertoire in the EAG, with a strengthened identity and more inclusive participation.

Conclusions

We started this chapter by stating that working with other individuals and organizations in development can be extremely challenging. We asked why it is so challenging, what kind of learning is required, and how it comes about. To answer the first two questions, we examined some of the ideas about inter-organizational relationships, participation and action learning. To answer the third question, we provided an account of creating an action learning space in the context of an environment and development intervention in Zimbabwe. There are a number of conclusions we can now draw:

- *With respect to inter-organizational relationships.* The case study we examined was a small-scale example. However, as we saw, the inter-organizational relationships were quite complex, with different organizations having different interests and perspectives. There were elements of coordination present both through the EAG and through the specific roles of the church-based group, the environmental NGO and the town council. There was also an element of competition for control of the project and over the widows. What the workshop aimed to do was to put the relationships on a more cooperative footing. Although the latter would have involved much more trust than it was possible to create in a single event, the tools for agenda setting helped to make explicit the agendas and interests of participants and thus to learn more about each other.

- *With respect to participation.* The workshop was an invited space for a group of people who had previously been excluded from discussions. However it also enabled the widows to exert citizenship and voice by making their demands on the council if they were to participate in the proposed project. Although one could not characterize this as radical citizenship, in that it did not have wider transformation effects, it was a kind of active citizenship that led to some realignment of relationships, reducing their dependence on the church-based group and establishing a direct link with the council.

- *With respect to action learning spaces.* This action learning space was deliberately created. However, many non-intentional opportunities for debate and dialogue present themselves within a politically educated populace. In this instance, the action learning was structured and steered, yet it was based on a set of social realities – social position, perceptions, needs and interests – some of which were common and some different. Much of the learning was through the expression and discussion of those differences through structured activity.

- *With respect to power.* In this microcosm, it is possible to see that power relations were both embedded and overt. While one would expect poor widows from a high density settlement to be in a relatively less powerful position than those in government, there were other less visible power relations – for example between the widows and the church-based group. In addition, although we had no obvious 'power over' or 'power to' as researchers, and were aiming to exert 'power with' (Rowlands, 1997), inevitably our own position as researchers had a kind of convening power.

- *With respect to communicative and strategic action.* To some extent, the workshop design tried to take into account both types of action in relation to the kinds of learning that were expected to take place. However, although conceptual distinctions are made, practices may be less clear. For example, the NGO might characterize its own approach as supporting communicative action, yet it also needs to obtain donor funding and may need to engage in strategic action to achieve it. There may thus be constant movement between types of action, depending on context and other players.

- *With respect to facilitation and mediation.* We were not experts in the use of participatory techniques. However, we did quite a bit of homework, engaged with actors beforehand, and tested our design before the workshop. The EAG created a relatively safe space for differences to be worked out.

What we have discussed and described in this chapter indicates the importance of learning in multi-stakeholder interventions and how learning can take place through contestation between actors. This alone does not lead to 'good' development or to positive outcomes. However, without it, 'good' development is less likely to be achieved.

Notes

1   Competition is used in the conventional market sense, with its attendant institutional framework; it is acknowledged, however, that competitors can be, and often are, interdependent. Coordination is seen as a hierarchical set of relationships with rules and regulations to achieve particular goals: examples are coordination by the state or by the UN. Contrary to the vertical aspect of coordination, cooperation is seen as a more horizontal set of relationships often, but not exclusively, associated with non-governmental, voluntary and community organizations.
2   In Chapter 2, we counterposed instrumental and communicative action. Habermas also has a third category – *strategic* action, which is oriented to the successful achievement of goals.
3   Note that the concept of 'community' was constantly used, but in different ways. As we have said elsewhere: 'the word "community" implies an identity between people by virtue of where they live, and their common characteristics and interests, it also hides their diversity' (Johnson and Wilson, 2000: 1899).

4 | Joint Learning through Similarity, Difference and Mutuality: North–South municipal partnerships[1]

Joint learning, often referred to as social learning, is similar in conception to communicative action. It usefully summarizes the idea of people engaging with one another for the explicit purpose of learning and co-producing knowledge for development. A consensus is emerging amongst different writers about the potential and limitations of joint learning. On one hand, there is significant agreement that a shared mindset – called 'background consensus' by Habermas, 'shared experience' by Nonaka (1994) and 'shared repertoire' by Wenger (1998) – is needed for productive engagement between actors. On the other hand, shared mindsets imply boundaries of inclusion and exclusion. Who is one of us and who is not one of us? Thus, for example, communities of practice, depending on the prior experience and repertoire shared by members, also exclude and potentially close down wider engagement and new kinds of learning.

We have also seen that, while similarity is needed for productive engagement, learning proceeds from difference. This became evident in the case study in Chapter 3. Of course, no two actors who purposefully engage in joint learning have identical mindsets and there are many levels of difference. There is nevertheless a tension between the two in social engagement.

Examination of what is required for joint learning also suggests a normative approach as something to promote. Yet, the normative and analytical are often intertwined and, if there is any sequence, the former tends to follow the latter. For example, when Lave and Wenger (1991) first introduced the term 'communities of practice', they were concerned to analyse how apprentices learned their trade, and especially its tacit knowledge dimensions, through learning from their more experienced peers. 'Communities of practice' thus began as an analytical concept, but Wenger later started to use it normatively as something to promote (Wenger 1998; Wenger *et al.*, 2002).

Even in the world of social engagement and development action, people do not tend to do things simply because they are 'right' or 'good', although such considerations enter the equation. Although values play an important role in social engagement, most people also require other incentives, especially if changes to established routines and practices are required. Whether at the individual or the organizational level, one needs to perceive that one is gaining something from the engagement, which, if it is to sustain itself, means mutual gains for the participating stakeholders.

This chapter explores these related issues of similarity, difference and incentives as they affected learning in two North–South municipal partnerships for development that were set up in the 1990s between Ugandan and UK local authorities. We start by describing the partnerships and their trajectories. Then we explore how learning was both facilitated and sometimes disabled in the partnerships, going on to examine incentives and mutuality, and the relationship between individual and organizational learning. We conclude the chapter with two small case studies that illustrate the interconnectedness of the challenges.

A tale of two partnerships: Kampala City Council and Kirklees Metropolitan Council; Iganga Town Council and Daventry District Council

The formation of North–South partnerships between urban municipalities in the mid-1990s was influenced by the 'brown agenda'/Agenda 21 emphasis on local action and by the decentralization agenda for good governance of major donors. Agenda

21 was the plan of action that derived from the 1992 United Nations Conference on Environment and Development (the first 'World Summit'), envisaging local government as a main actor. The 'brown agenda' is that part of Agenda 21 that concerns creating a sustainable urban environment, addressing issues such as water, sanitation, solid waste management, air pollution and traffic management (Bartone *et al.*, 1994). Decentralization has also focused on local government: transferring state activity to this level was seen as a way of making it more accountable to its citizens, as well as strengthening service delivery (World Bank, 2003: 187). A third aspect of Agenda 21 was that it envisaged a way forward through partnerships.

The partnerships that are our concern in this chapter are between UK and Ugandan municipalities. They were brokered initially by organizations such as the UK Local Government International Bureau and received funds for projects from the EU, the Commonwealth Local Government Forum and, in the case of the Kampala–Kirklees partnership featured here, from the World Bank. The aims of these partnerships, when they were initially funded by the European Union, focused on knowledge transfer from North to South of approaches, practices, tools, techniques and skills. Thus they included technical assistance from the UK, training and work experience attachments for Ugandans in the UK, local projects to improve the urban environment and services in Uganda, and community/NGO/local government linkages to support service delivery and increase community participation. It was also suggested that projects should build on examples of good practice in both South and North (Pasteur, 1998: 22–3).

These aims rested on two further assumptions, one methodological and one aspirational. The methodological assumption was that learning would take place through Northern and Southern professionals working together in a 'practitioner-to-practitioner' relationship. Such an assumption is based on the idea of professional equivalence and relative parity of status, and that officers from partner authorities would share knowledge and ideas on a collegial basis. The aspirational assumption was that there would be learning benefits to both North and South – in other words, mutual gains.

It was expected, however, that the learning benefits might be of different types. For example, a conference of the Local Government International Bureau on Uganda–UK partnerships in 2002 emphasized that the benefits were principally 'soft' and personal for Northern participants, including greater cultural awareness, friendship, mutual understanding and learning. However, Rossiter notes that Northern partners also have the potential to benefit in other ways: by adapting Southern participation processes, especially those practised by the NGO sector; learning from innovations in decentralized government in the South; adapting Southern anti-poverty agendas to the Northern context; and learning about poor community coping and self-reliance strategies, as well as user involvement in service provision in the South (2000: 26–7). Rossiter's point is important, because it takes us beyond diffuse personal learning in the North to 'hard' gains in terms of what is needed for a local authority to improve the way it goes about its core business, which is to provide services to its own citizens and taxpayers. It is in these terms that a partnership between local authorities must ultimately be justified if it is to survive.

The two partnerships on which we focus were both established in 1995. One was between the City Council of Kampala, the capital of Uganda with a population of about 2 million, and Kirklees Metropolitan Council in northern England, delivering services to about 750,000 people. Partnership activities in Kampala were located mainly in a Project Coordination Unit, a strategic 'think-tank' within the Council funded by the World Bank. The partnership ended in 2002 when its World Bank funding ended after two renewals.

The other partnership matched Iganga Town Council, a town in Eastern Uganda with a daytime population of about 50,000, with Daventry District Council in the English Midlands, which covers a large rural area as well as the small town from which it derives its name. A financial crisis in 2000 ended Daventry District Council's formal involvement in the partnership, but a 'Friends of Iganga' group was set up in the town to continue it. Daventry officers, current and retired, still work on Iganga projects in their own time through the 'Friends' (which also raises money). The Council also continues to host study visits by officers from Uganda.

Both partnerships focused primarily on environmental (or public) health, although issues such as financial management and planning were included. In the Iganga–Daventry partnership, environmental health referred mainly to waste management, storm water drainage, clean water supply and health promotion in Iganga. In the Kampala–Kirklees partnership involvement was mainly with waste management and traffic management in Kampala, as well as an evaluation input by Kirklees into the rehabilitation of the Kampala main drain. Although there were no practical projects in the UK, officers in Uganda had the opportunity to experience and comment on work carried out by the UK councils during their visits. UK officers in turn had the experience (the first for many) of trying to marry their developed country experience and practice with the limited resources available for environmental health infrastructure and practice in Uganda.

World Bank funding of the Kampala–Kirklees partnership covered time spent by Kirklees officers on the projects. The relatively modest funding for projects in the Iganga–Daventry partnership ruled out a similar arrangement. The Kampala–Kirklees partnership was also based on contracts and more tightly interpreted by the two councils than that between Daventry and Iganga. In the latter, the Memorandum of Understanding for the partnership included building community links, none of which occurred in Kampala–Kirklees. Establishing 'Friends of Iganga' in Daventry to continue the partnership after the Council financial crisis in 2000 can be seen as an extension of these community links and a parallel group ('Friends of Daventry') has since been established in Iganga.

Although the Kampala-Kirklees partnership was more tightly bounded than the Iganga–Daventry partnership, informal as well as formal processes of partnership characterized both of them. Alongside building professional trust by working together, friendships and one-to-one relationships were built, and maintained by letter and e-mail outside the visits made in both directions by officers and some politicians. Despite, or because of, this process, as well as other reasons we return to below, the Kampala–Kirklees partnership stopped in 2002, while, as mentioned above, the Iganga–Daventry partnership is now sustained through non-governmental links.

Common mindsets: a necessary but insufficient basis for joint learning?

Our empirical research consisted of semi-structured interviews with environmental health officers, associated engineers and other key officers and politicians in the four councils. We also interviewed civil society and private sector groups as appropriate. Finally, we wrote reports for, and held feedback workshops or meetings with, each of the four participating councils to present, discuss and revise our preliminary findings.

Both UK and Ugandan environmental health officers and related engineers who participated in these practitioner-to-practitioner partnerships endorsed the idea that shared mindsets and shared repertoires enable productive engagement. As they reflected on their participation and their relationships with counterparts, comments included: 'We spoke the same language' . . . 'We treated problems at the same level' . . . 'You can share ideas' . . . 'You're from the same profession'.

There are two aspects to this commonality. One is that, in the UK and Uganda, these officers had received similar higher education and professional training. The second, broader aspect was that they shared a practical, problem-solving mindset that is often associated with professional practice. On the face of it, therefore, they established easily that shared lifeworld or 'background consensus' that may lie behind all narrative exchange. This meant, basically, that there was a strong foundation for trust between the officers. They could bounce proposals, share thoughts and interrogate each other's ideas without fear of appearing ridiculous or stupid. They could engage in something approaching Habermas's notion of communicative action, involving:

> interpersonal communication which is oriented towards mutual understanding and in which other participants are treated as genuine persons, not as objects of manipulation. Actors do not primarily aim at their own success, but want to harmonize their action plans with the other participants. (Huttunen and Heikkinen, 1998: 311)

Yet a shared mindset did not in itself guarantee trust and communicative action between the officers. A Daventry engineer thus observed: 'It felt very strange to start with, trying to explain what we did. It was a bit lukewarm because it was such a strange thing to do.' What also seemed necessary was a shared experience, as elaborated by Nonaka (1994) and Weick (1995: 188–9), which grew through repeated engagement (Vangen and Huxham, 2003) while working together on projects. Weick suggests that developing shared experience reinforces a positive self-identity among similar mindsets, such as those of professionals. It is also self-reinforcing – each reinforcement of positive self-identity is an incentive for extending the shared experience. Weick further argues that shared experience in 'doing' together is in fact more important than prior shared meanings (1995: 188–9).

In Iganga–Daventry, shared experience was consolidated by building friendships and becoming involved in each others' family and social networks, reinforced in both towns by links to community organizations which grew up around the partnership. Thus here multiple ties developed that drove repeated exchanges. They were described by one Iganga officer as having 'tied a lot of strings. If one string goes, there will be another string to hold it in place.' In Iganga–Daventry there was both a professional deepening of the shared experience through joint projects (one Daventry engineer commented that there was nothing like standing in a storm drain together with your counterpart for deepening bonds) and a broadening through friendships and community ties.

Building shared experience was not so straightforward in Kampala–Kirklees. Workshops did help, but the tight, contractual interpretation of the partnership meant engagements and shared experiences did not broaden beyond the officers in their professional roles. The professional relationship seemed also to be characterized by discontinuities rather than repeated exchange. This became manifested as frustration, especially by Kirklees officers, because of poor communication and lack of feedback about progress on projects or in response to evaluations and advice. These officers felt increasingly, as the partnership progressed, that they were being treated 'like consultants' who held expert knowledge to provide answers to Kampala questions. This also mirrored the World Bank's construction of the partnership as a form of inexpensive consultancy involving one-way knowledge transfers from North to South, through frequently conceptualizing the work done by Kirklees as technical assistance or technical assessment. Even when Kampala put forward its own ideas, the World Bank response would be, according to one Kirklees officer: 'What does Kirklees think?'

Difference and learning

Difference is a double-edged sword. On one hand, it is the source of joint learning – one compares and contrasts what one knows with what others know. In this way one can learn through the other knowledges with which one engages. Ideally, as we have suggested, there is also potential to construct new knowledge together by learning *with* the other actors.

On the other hand, difference signifies an unequal relation between people and therefore potentially a power relation. Inequalities and power relations can be manifested in many ways, but of primary concern to us is the way they relate to knowledge engagements between actors. To a large extent, the two partnerships showed that perceptions and practices of learning were based on the idea of joint problem definition and solution through engagement of the different knowledges of the participants. Part of the difference between UK and Ugandan municipalities was in relation to technical knowledge. UK officers, for example, knew about correct use of equipment or computer technologies in engineering design, and in this sense they were partly teachers with specialist knowledge to transfer. This knowledge was also perceived at a different level, where the UK officers were seen by their Ugandan counterparts, and by themselves to some extent, as exponents of 'best practice'. Information gathering and organization, public engagement and managing expectations, work organization and time management were variously cited in this respect. One Iganga officer stated, 'What you see in Daventry is a model; when you come back you strive to reach certain levels.' And a senior Kampala officer referred to Kirklees's model of structure and accompanying practices as something he would like to see in Kampala. Thus UK best practice represented, in the Foucauldian sense, a 'truth' of how things should be done.

By contrast, Ugandan officers were seen by both sides of each partnership as having the experiential knowledge of local context and conditions. Thus, a Kampala engineer commented: 'Local knowledge is very important with respect to traffic: what works in Kirklees does not necessarily work here.' Moreover, others were more sceptical about Northern models. One Iganga officer said that Iganga was a 'bit far' from Daventry in terms of relating to it as a model, and another specified institutional constraints (such as lack of finance and political support) on the applicability of UK models. In Kampala, the limits to which the Kirklees model could be applied were used to explain why the Council approached

Hyderabad, an authority from another developing country, for a new partnership after the Kirklees partnership ended.

It is a moot point whether knowledge of 'best practice' and knowledge of context were valued equally, although both UK and Ugandan officers voiced their respect for the knowledge of their counterparts. Some UK officers were also overtly concerned not to assume that they had a better knowledge. As one retired Daventry officer commented: 'The main obstacles were the ability to leave all the baggage behind in terms of the way we do things. We have assumptions about our expertise and a tendency to "tell".' Others, however, saw themselves to some extent as teachers: a Daventry engineer thought it was like working alongside others and teaching at the same time, while an officer from Kirklees saw his role in a clearly educational light, stating, 'It's a bit like taking two trainees and building them up.'

Of course, the UK knowledge of best practice had itself been derived from experience and reinforced by routine enactment. This, however, was something Ugandan officers were often unable to do in their everyday working lives because of resource and time constraints. Nevertheless, the comment above about traffic management suggests that at least one Ugandan officer recognized the contextual base of the UK officers' knowledge of 'best practice'. In general, however, the Ugandan officers' knowledge of context was mainly used to interpret and adapt UK 'best practice', a process which Entwistle (1997) has summarized as strategic learning.

We have seen that for Entwistle strategic learning is part of a continuum between surface and deep learning. Surface learning involves assimilating the perceived superior knowledge of the other and attempting to reproduce it in practice. An example of this was Iganga Town Council's early attempt to replicate the Daventry individual household refuse collection model. Exact replication was impossible for a variety of reasons, from low capacity to maintain the refuse collection truck to the impossibility of penetrating many residential areas in Iganga with a vehicle. Iganga Town Council learned from the experience, however, and household collection was replaced by a skip system. This was an example of strategic learning to adapt the Daventry model, or single-loop learning.

In these circumstances, and despite aspirations in this regard, possibilities for 'deep' or 'double-loop' learning – what Kolb (1984) calls a transformation of experience where problems are reframed – are limited. Thus, a capacity to reframe problems was certainly what Kirklees officers hoped to gain out of their partnership with Kampala (see below), and in this sense an unequal knowledge–power relationship was of little use to them. It certainly contributed to their perception of being treated like consultants.

Beyond unequal knowledge–power relationships there was possibly another limiting factor on deep learning and consequent reframing of problems. This limit arose because of the similarities between the officers discussed above, particularly the similar mindsets of the actors in the engagement. As practitioner-to-practitioner, the partnerships excluded other mindsets, and as a result they never threw off the 'comfort blanket', as one Kirklees engineer put it.

In themselves, however, the distinctions of surface, strategic and deep might not be so significant in so far as reproducing, adapting and transforming knowledge and practices all have a place in learning processes, and may meet local government goals in a range of ways. The main dilemma is the extent to which possibilities might be denied because of (1) the exclusionary boundaries imposed by the need for shared repertoires/experiences/consensus; and (2) unequal valuing of prior knowledges within the learning engagements.

Incentives and disincentives

A stated incentive for the partnerships was the potential for mutual professional development. In particular, the projects enabled Ugandan officers to apply their theoretical learning and build on it through on-the-job experience. The comparative lack of such opportunities was seen as a major issue in Uganda where resources are limited and officers spend considerable time on general tasks and administration rather than building their professional expertise through practice.

One officer in Iganga pointed out that professional contacts were extended, while an officer from Kampala underlined the importance of the hands-on approach. The projects included finance for two-way visits, so that officers could work alongside each other in both the UK and Uganda. The visits also enabled the Ugandan officers to tap into other learning sources available in the UK local authorities.

For UK officers an important incentive was described as the professional challenge, which relates to Weick's reinforcement of positive self-identity (1995: 188–9). The projects gave these officers the opportunity to work in a context where they were taken 'back to basics' in terms of their professional expertise. One Kirklees officer said: 'In the UK we tend to work to the book. In Uganda we often had to throw the book away and work from first principles.' A Daventry engineer also observed how much of their work in the UK concerns marginal improvements to infrastructure, while working in Uganda took them back to the nineteenth-century origins of their profession in areas such as public health, and hence to some of the fundamental human purposes of engineering.

A key incentive for both Uganda and UK officers to participate in the partnership related to learning in terms of core business. On the Uganda side, both Kampala and Iganga officers indicated that this was to a large extent fulfilled. They learned not only technical skills, but also skills that relate to practice generally. They therefore compared the practitioner-to-practitioner relationship favourably with consultancy (to which they were more accustomed). One Iganga officer expressed it thus:

> In the traditional technical help an expert comes to manage a project for a limited period. The expert comes with a huge budget.

Then there is a counterpart who is very under-funded. The expert does not understand why things are delayed, and comes with the missionary zeal of someone who knows the answers. The relationship with the counterpart thus becomes fraught.

Incentives can easily become undermined, however, if capacity is built in areas of practice, but the financial and other resources aren't available to sustain them beyond and outside of the time-limited partnership projects. Noting that capacity had been built among officers in engaging with the public, a Kampala politician stated:

> We have tried [to involve the public in solid waste management] but KCC may not have the capacity: for example, we may tell people to take the garbage to the skip and people may do it, but then it gets full and overflows and people get defeated. This is because of lack of resources. People can respond very easily but usually they get disappointed because we can't sustain these projects.

In addition, officers involved in the partnerships were seen as privileged by the experience, which could mean, as in Iganga, that they were expected to take on even more responsibility for the delivery of results on their return from visits to Daventry, although not usually supported by resources.

In Kirklees, too, the espoused theory that differentiated the practitioner-to-practitioner methodology from consultancy was qualified somewhat. As we have seen, a Kirklees criticism of their partnership with Kampala was exactly their growing sense that they were being treated like consultants. For these officers, the incentive was also the desire to learn in terms of core business, partly driven by UK local government policy that encourages officers to challenge what they are doing in order to learn new and effective ways of practising, to 'think out of the box', as the Kirklees engineer quoted above commented. The partnership was seen as one way of doing such learning, and it worked to a certain extent for, when discussing a knotty problem on their home turf,

Kirklees Highways engineers would still say to one another after the partnership ended, 'If we were in Kampala, we would do it this way.'

The discontinuities between visits and lack of communication to which we referred above, however, meant that for the Kirklees officers it did not work well enough in terms of mutual learning. In Weick's terms there was a failure to enact the partnership, and with it ongoing opportunities for reflection and reinforcement of positive self-identity were lost to a significant extent. One Kirklees Highways engineer, lamenting this loss, concluded that the partnership should have been 'personal development for us as well as for them'.

Individual and organizational learning

So far we have concentrated on the learning by the individual officers who were involved in the partnerships. A key dimension for the local authorities who employed them, however, would be the organizational benefits of this individual learning.

Peter Senge, writing on organizational learning, has noted that 'if teams learn, they become a microcosm for learning throughout the organization' (1990: 236). In other words the mechanism for organizational learning depends on the engagement of individuals *within* the organization. Such engagement, however, involves its own power relations. Hierarchy and power can act as a potential inhibitor of sharing knowledge and therefore of changing practice. On one hand, experiential knowledge may be a source of power for those who hold it, both higher up and lower down in the hierarchy, and may not therefore be shared. On the other hand, those higher up may not want their ways of doing things challenged, or may not be prepared to provide the resources to allow such knowledge sharing.

In practice, the four local authorities had difficulties building a learning culture around the partnerships, and sharing and embedding the learning organizationally. There are a number of dimensions to this issue. First, there is the place and role of the practitioners in their respective organizations. This was particularly noticeable in Kampala City Council, where the Project Coordination Unit (PCU) became a repository of knowledge and expertise that was difficult to share with traditional departments. Moreover this difficulty was not simply a technical communication problem, as was stressed by one senior Kampala politician:

> There are some weaknesses with that unit. Most Heads of traditional departments [HoDs] are against it. They think it is against the HoDs, that it is the Think Tank with too-wise men. There is some lack of cooperation, but they should work with it. Also that unit is looked after by the World Bank, with better remuneration and resources. For example, there are no computers on the desks in the traditional departments, yet they are on everybody's desk in the PCU, so there is perhaps some jealousy.

Personal communications with the head of the PCU, after this research was undertaken, suggested that it was endeavouring to share learning through a mentoring system and also trying to develop more interface between different project teams. However, this process was subject to a further structural constraint in that the partnership focused on projects which provided opportunities for Ugandan officers to practise, but undermined wider changes because their very specific focus means they are not susceptible to knowledge sharing in the way that ongoing national programmes may be.

The challenge of embedding learning and using it to rethink practice was also limited in the Northern councils. Although within both Daventry and Kirklees councils officers had shared some of their learning across professional barriers, this process could at best be described as patchy and not routine.

Second, there are political and resource constraints. Changes in ruling politicians can impact on the continuity of the practitioner-to-practitioner partnership. Also, the motivation to capitalize on the learning from partnerships can diminish with changes in the membership of the governing councils. Finally, even if there is a strong learning culture in a local authority, it may not conceptualize partnerships (whether North–South or not) for this purpose.

The task of sharing and embedding the learning beyond the specific units or individuals involved was thus difficult. Senge's suggestion, quoted above, may be a necessary but not sufficient process.

Making the connections

Previous sections of this chapter have suggested an analytical framework for joint learning based on (1) similar and different knowledges (including surface-strategic-deep learning); (2) incentives and disincentives (including positive identity); and (3) linking individual to organizational learning. In order to capture the complex reality of the group learning process of these partnerships, however, the interplay between these elements is important. In short, we need to move from a factor to a process analysis.

Two of the partnership projects illustrate this: traffic management in central Kampala and water, hygiene and housing in Iganga. Both demonstrate the playing out in practice of the engagement of different knowledges, and that, despite the qualifiers we have noted above being present in these examples, there were elements too of deep/transformational learning. We look at each in turn.

Traffic management in central Kampala
The problem of traffic congestion in Kampala was conceived as requiring road regulation and public education – or changes in driver, pedestrian, kerb-side trader and police behaviour – as well as road maintenance. The model was derived from the UK, where there is a high degree of regulation and user conformity. The process of arriving at and designing a demonstration project based on traffic filtering at a particularly busy junction involved reflec-

tion and challenge by both Kampala and Kirklees officers. One dimension was the nature of the tools and techniques required to investigate the problem and design a solution. For the Kampala officers, hands-on traffic observation and measurement were culturally, as well as instrumentally, new, whereas the Kirklees officers just went and did it to 'get a feel'. Kampala officers also learnt how to use a computer package for designing regulated traffic flow. However in defining the problem, and engaging in processes to resolve it, both Kirklees and Kampala officers faced learning challenges. These were expressed by a Kirklees transport engineer as follows:

> They [Kampala City Council – KCC] . . . wanted to clear the hawkers off the streets. We said, 'Can you do that?' They said, 'No.' We said, 'Keep away from them. If you can't deliver you're wasting your time, you need to take people with you. You need stakeholder engagement so you need to talk to them, because they hold KCC in very low esteem.' And KCC learned something – as well as the techniques.
>
> We all made assumptions that weren't right. But we had made those assumptions as the [Kampala–Kirklees] team. We overlaid some European assumptions. Some were challenged by our counterparts, some were not. Some worked, some did not. For example, there was a cultural problem with the police. . . . We borrowed 15 policemen to make it work, but the chief of police turned up and said he didn't want his officers doing this. He was totally anti. We persuaded him to try it. Then at a meeting later with the traffic police he had come round to it.

This account highlights the value placed on shared experience (assumptions were made as a Kampala–Kirklees team), but also reveals some deep-seated knowledge differences between Kampala and Kirklees officers about practice. Thus:

- Kirklees officers would observe a congested junction to get a tacit feel for what was happening, but for Kampala officers this was not a normal practice.

- Kirklees officers would keep away from things they knew they couldn't enact, whereas Kampala offices thought of practice as what they ideally wanted to do.

- Kirklees officers wanted to experiment on the ground, but the Kampala chief of police initially didn't want his officers used in this way.

Such observations, with their undertones of cultural difference, qualify the idea of shared professional mindsets. Indeed it probably makes sense to think of people having multiple mindsets that are based on profession, social position, geographical location and so on. Some mindsets of the Kampala and Kirklees officers were shared, but others were very different.

The Kirklees officer who gave this account claimed that his Kampala counterparts 'learned something' from these differences, and Kampala engineers commented on learning about practice from Kirklees. There were also obvious incentives – for Kampala officers in terms of their learning about how to approach problems as well as the techniques, for Kirklees officers about the professional challenge of going back to basics. However, whether practices learned through this project have become institutionalized over time is not known.

The actual highways solutions that were implemented in Kampala were technical changes to junctions, and could not be described as embodying deep learning. There were hints, however, that the Kirklees officers went through a transformational or deep learning process in relation to the UK, moving from an 'educating' to a 'working with' conceptualization of public engagement. Referring to engagements with a wide group of stakeholders, including a workshop that he and a colleague initiated in Kampala, the officer quoted above continued:

> We have re-thought our public engagement. No longer is it, here is an engineering problem and a solution and this is how we're going to do it. We had had some experiences here [in the UK] our-

selves, but having to go through that process of getting people on board has made you realize how important it is here. . . . For example, we wanted to put a bus lane on one of our roads [in Kirklees]. We were able to get local people to support us – the community, the disabled. . . . This is a better way and it questions the whole foundations on which you stand.

Surface, strategic and deep learning are, in this example, fluid categories and it is quite possible for one kind to lead to the other in a different context. A good deal of confidence, indeed a positive conception of one's professional identity, is required, however, to question the 'whole foundations on which you stand'. One can envisage how such a positive self-identity might be present among the Kirklees engineers, reinforced through years of practice, not to mention invitations from the World Bank to participate in this partnership. The Kampala officers, in contrast, would have had far fewer opportunities during their careers to reinforce their positive identity as practising engineers. Consequently they might feel uncomfortable, for example, with observing at a road junction in order to get a feel, the tacit dimensions of which might suggest that codified engineering principles are not enough to solve a problem.

Water, hygiene and housing in Iganga

This was a funded project to address poor public health conditions in a village on the outskirts of Iganga town. Problem definition initially involved the Iganga public health inspector adapting Daventry tools and techniques – a housing survey form to which he added questions of interest to Iganga. Town council officers were trained to deliver and tabulate the survey. A Daventry environmental health officer continues the story:

With the people who did the survey, we analysed [the data] and asked what were the problems and what could be done, so we had a good idea in advance of what was needed. Those who did the survey did the analysis. We just went round prompting.

The village chairman organized a public meeting, which took

place under a tree the next day. We mentioned each item in the survey results and asked questions. For example, 'Why are there only five toilets?' People came up with various answers, such as lack of money or skills to build them. One woman said her husband was always drunk and incapable of building a latrine. Then we asked about possible remedies and she said 'put him in jail and when he's sober make him dig latrines!'

We also asked why the children were not being inoculated. They said that the clinic was too far, and when you got there it did not always have the drugs. The remedy was to bring the clinic to them.

At the end we said we would provide water protection and immunization if they improved their houses.

This example shows in summary form part of the learning process involved in defining problems and seeking solutions. The adaptation of UK survey forms can be seen as strategic learning for the purposes of gathering information on Iganga health conditions. However the process turned into a small piece of participatory action research, without any of the officers having been trained in such a process or having used it before.

To some extent, therefore, even though some of the tools and processes were adaptations of existing practices, officers in both Iganga and Daventry reframed their ideas about how to analyse the problem and arrive at a solution. However, their evaluation of the learning process shows different perceptions of the value of their respective contributions. For example, the public health inspector in Iganga said that he used to believe that public health problems were a matter for the Council – Daventry 'showed him' that the public should see public health as their problem too. His perception was that the principles of best practice were thus provided by Daventry (even though the process had involved contributions from both sides). One Daventry EHO supported the UK best practice/Uganda knowledge of local context thesis ('We did transfer from our skills; they transferred things back from their community links'), but another had a different perception: '[Daventry officers] did seminars in the council so that Iganga could see what people do in Daventry in terms of communicating with the community. . . . But Daventry [District Council] people learnt more from this as Iganga [Town Council] people do it better (for example, through plays). We tend to assume that we know best, but we don't.' In this instance, thus, the value placed on Iganga knowledge was not simply about context but about ways of doing, and it challenged officers in both Daventry and Iganga to reflect on their current practices.

That said, however, as with the Kampala traffic management example, the persistence of the practices recorded in this example is not clear beyond the project. This model of defining problems in water, hygiene and housing had not been pursued in other parts of Iganga at the time of our study. Organizational learning from bounded, funded projects is indeed rather difficult when the dedicated funds are not available to replicate. In Weick's terminology, if ongoing enactment of a practice is difficult because of resource constraints, the incentive to do so will eventually disappear.

Inevitably, we cannot make general statements about practitioner-to-practitioner learning from the two illustrations above. There were unidirectional elements, but generally the process was characterized for the individual participating officers on both sides by a dialogic quality, critical questioning, adapting ideas and practices, and exposure to new, but shared, experiences and ways of doing. Certainly these two cases involved many more elements of Senge's team learning and Wenger's communities of practice than would be usual, say, in a conventional North–South consultancy arrangement. For both the individuals and their organizations, however, it is obviously difficult to maintain an ongoing virtuous cycle of reflection and enactment, and therefore sustained learning and practice.

Conclusion

This chapter has drawn on some of the concepts we introduced in Chapter 2 – Habermas's notion of shared lifeworlds/background consensus and the place of commonality (or similarity) and difference in learning through social engagement and development action. The chapter has also drawn on ideas of communities of practice, different types of learning, and the challenges of connecting individual, team and organizational learning. In this case study, the contribution of self-identity and shared mindsets and how they are built or reinforced through the practice of shared activity to make sense of difference (Weick, 1995) were important explanatory variables in the successful dimensions of these partnerships. However 'difference', although a key source of learning, was also a source of inequality, in turn a potential obstacle to transformative outcomes. It remains one of the biggest contradictions in learning for development.

Note

1 This chapter is an adaptation of an article that first appeared as G. Wilson and H. Johnson (2007), 'Knowledge, learning and practice in North–South municipal partnerships', *Local Government Studies*, 33 (2): 253–69.

5 | Changing the Self and Changing the Organization: doing things better and doing them differently

In previous chapters, we have examined everyday learning amongst different stakeholders in development interventions: the different knowledges, practices and engagements of actors trying to work in partnership. In each case, processes of learning to do things better and differently were identified, as well as the challenges that such learning presents.

In this chapter, we are going to examine more formal learning arrangements: the experience of people who set out to become 'better' in the field of development policy and management by participating in study programmes. Development policy and management include different elements: development as a field of study and action; processes of policy development; intervention and its management; and participation more broadly in enterprise that contributes to income generation, employment and the many dimensions of well-being across a country's population.

There are a number of reasons for becoming 'better' at development policy and management. One is the failure of much intervention. Partly because of this, and partly because of the influence of conventional management in development organizations, there has been a process of professionalization amongst those working in development organizations and an increasing awareness of the need for different kinds of expertise, from organizational and financial skills to research and project management capabilities. Such skills have been in demand within private enterprises too. In parallel, there has been an increase in the number of development 'experts' or private consultants. We have commented briefly on the latter within the context of learning in and through North–South partnerships, in which (whether rightly or wrongly) the role of consultants was unfavourably compared to practitioner-to-practitioner learning methodologies.

Learning to engage better and differently, make better decisions, and contribute to better policy development are an important part of work-based professionalism, and of aligning development processes more closely to need and positive outcomes. However, such processes do not depend simply on what individuals do. How individuals relate to and work in their organizations, and how their organizations function internally and within their social-economic settings, are crucial to effective social engagement. Thus, as we have noted in previous chapters, how individual learning becomes institutionalized and whether organizations behave differently as a result may determine their potential for promoting transformation. While change is often thrust on individuals and organizations by forces beyond their control, the ability to exert greater influence and to achieve shared social goals is an important organizational or collective asset in the face of powerful institutions and policies that might present obstacles to 'good change'.

For such reasons (as well as the more instrumental ones around taking advantage of new 'educational markets') there has been a substantial increase in education and training programmes for development policy and management to build knowledge, understanding and capabilities in particular areas of expertise. Yet research into the impact of such programmes on individuals and organizations in the development field – which triggered the investigations informing this chapter – has been limited.

The chapter focuses on development managers who have undertaken further studies to improve their knowledge, understanding and professional capabilities and skills. By development managers we include all those who are working professionally in development organizations (whether government ministries, bi- or multilateral aid agencies, international and national NGOs, consultancy companies, or forms of advocacy and campaigning). We also include those who have development management roles in private enterprise that contributes to or works closely with countries in the global South (be it manufacture, marketing, international banks, *et cetera*). Overall, we are concerned with those who are potential change agents within organizations that have external social goals as well as internal ones, even if those organizations would not necessarily be considered to be in the frontline of development action.

Conceptualizing the terrain

Despite the considerable challenges to the success of interventions in development, there has been a phenomenal increase in the number of development organizations and development professionals. Their role in development has been the subject of the participation debate, as we have discussed in previous chapters, and there are considerable challenges in straddling the different lifeworlds of well-meaning interveners and those whose lives are subject to such interventions (Borda-Rodriguez, 2008).

So an important question is: how can development action be undertaken in a better or different way? The participation debate has obviously had this question in mind. The Habermasian concept of communicative action and the bringing together of different types of knowledge interests (technical, hermeneutic and emancipatory), together with the need to challenge power relations embedded in dominant development 'truths' (Foucault), underline a big agenda for development action – one that many development professionals may find rather daunting.

The conceptual frameworks – or big ideas – that we raised in Chapter 2 were accompanied by middle-range ideas about learning as a process. In particular we examined learning as the social construction of knowledge (which may reflect the power relations in which it is constructed); learning as a situated process emerging from the interactions of people and context (also influenced by the social relations of those contexts); and learning as generalized knowledge that can be applied to many situations and contexts (for example, the presumed universalism of engineering principles).

A theme threading through Chapter 2 and subsequent chapters is that of transformation: whether as an outcome of Habermas's communicative action or of the types of learning outlined by Entwistle or Kolb's experiential/action learning. As we have noted, transformation can characterize individual and joint or organizational learning. In the second case, we have examined the roles of communities of practice and teams and processes of conversational learning.

Underlying all our discussion of joint learning is the need, on one hand, for common, shared ground and trust, and, on the other, for difference as a trigger for learning. The tension around difference is the spectrum between 'different and equal' and 'different and more or less powerful'.

This final point provides us with the launchpad for the role, education and training of those working professionally in development – the development managers who are the focus of this chapter. One of the tensions for development management is whether, on one hand, it could or should be characterized as having continuities with colonial administration (Kothari, 2006), and thus with historically constituted power relations, or, on the other, whether it is a challenge to the past and has transformative potential by building on 'different and equal'. While the answer to that question might rather obviously be 'it depends', a positive outcome would require formal education and training for those working in development to be highly reflective and to promote awareness and understanding of the past as well as the present. Thus in addition to the frameworks, concepts, tools, techniques and skills that are needed to make better policies, decisions and interventions, such education and training would include an understanding of colonialism, different theories of development and underdevelopment, and the role of economic, social and political domination as manifested in the past, changing over time and persisting in the present. In other words, it requires a thorough and critical examination of development 'truths'.

The organizational and institutional arena of those engaging in education and training is also a key consideration for teachers, trainers and course participants. There are a number of dimensions. First are the place and role of international development organizations, in particular in Southern countries, and the extent to which there is social engagement on equal terms. Second, there is the relationship between such organizations and their national offices. While the localization of such organizations has been a growing trend, the relationship between 'head' and 'local' office is also a site for scrutiny of both the development and control of policy and the potential acculturation of organizational purposes and behaviours. Third is the existence of many national development organizations, and particularly the multiplication of NGOs, including consultancy organizations, in many Southern countries. An issue, in relation to this third point, is whether and how such organizations differ philosophically and ideologically from their international or Northern counterparts (if one can describe them as such) or instead reflect an internationalization of a common or similar perspective on development action. Finally, to the extent that development organizations are indeed a reconfigured form, having continuities with colonial administration, the need for reflection and reflexiveness becomes even more imperative, as we have noted above.

Standing back, studying and relating to different ideas and practices, and gaining new skills, can be mechanisms for new thinking. But such processes need to be located in a critical reflection on whether professionalism, tools, techniques and skills are replacing the need for a political and social awareness that yields knowledge and insight into other contexts. In fact, Kothari argues that professionalism and expertise have displaced in-depth country knowledge in development practice (2006: 248). On the other hand, we should not doubt the need for tools, techniques and skills. The frequent lack of capacities at middle and upper levels of analysis, policy making and implementation, and the institutional settings in which such capacities can become capabilities, is still a challenge for development and for formal learning – issues to which we now turn.

Formal learning and action learning

One constructivist definition of learning in education is: 'an active process in which meanings are constructed by the learner as they interact with the course materials, each other and their teachers, and internalize the substance of the teaching they encounter' (Atkins *et al.*, 2002: 124, italics in original). This perspective assumes that participants need 'to *transform* their existing knowledge, and integrate old and new knowledge in ways that demonstrate a personal grasp and the ability to apply their knowledge and skills to new contexts and practices' (*ibid.*, italics in original). The process of application is, of course, particularly crucial to development action. Application can mean many things, however: from becoming more reflective about one's work and its place in development, to using tools and techniques to do things differently, to directly influencing policy direction in one's organization, as well as wider advocacy.

The included of learning propounded by the education programmes involved in the research behind this chapter are based on constructivist approaches, in particular the idea of creating 'reflective practitioners'. The idea of a reflective practitioner derives both from Schön's (1983) book of the same name and from the ideas of learning that we drew from Kolb in Chapter 2. First, Schön suggested that learning was not linear application of knowledge to situations – learning first and application second. Rather it involved an iterative process of learning through practice and reflection on practice, particularly amongst working professionals. This is quite similar to Kolb's ideas of experiential learning. It also has some similarities to the ideas of learning proposed by

Wenger – which we have also addressed in earlier chapters. Wenger noted that learning was the 'engine of practice' (1998: 96).

In this chapter we are also interested in what happens within organizations as a result of individual learning – in whether formal learning leads both to better individual practitioners and to better organizational engagement with development. This is of course a profound question and our study only scratched the surface. To make this preliminary foray, we referred to the ideas of Argyris and Schön (1996) discussed earlier, particularly (1) the *mismatches* between learning and practice and how practice might change as a result; (2) the idea of single-loop learning in which individuals and organizations might learn to do things *better*; and (3) the idea of double-loop learning in which individuals and organizations might learn to do things *differently*.

In the first study that we refer to in the sections that follow, we counterposed two models of how professional learning is applied: a linear model of study leading to direct application or particular learning to one's own work; and an action learning model, involving the interaction of individual learning with other individual and organizational experience. Such learning might lead, we hypothesized, to possible key transformative moments when such interactions became a catalyst for doing things differently (as opposed to doing things better). We found, of course, that both models applied, and that, indeed, it was not always easy to distinguish between them. We also reflected on whether and how course participants formed 'communities of practice' (Wenger, 1998). Did they share common concerns? Did they produce new meaning collectively? Did they develop new shared repertoires of skills? Did they consolidate those into new forms of practice? Again, we only have very partial answers – but thinking about these issues took us beyond the individual and organization to thinking about how development actors can work collectively to challenge and reflect more widely, joining up across organizations and contexts. This is a particularly important question in terms of the kinds of issues raised by Kothari about development professionals: is there a reconfiguration occurring at a broad level amongst them? To what extent are continuities being individually or collectively challenged and how? These questions were also addressed by the second investigation we come to below, and, while we do not have clear answers from our investigation, they are crucial issues for professionals working in development.

Doing things better (and differently?): individual learning experiences

The first investigation was a study carried out in 2001–2 into the impact of four postgraduate programmes in development policy and management (Ayele *et al.*, 2002; Johnson and Thomas, 2003, 2004 and 2007). The programmes promoted learning 'on the job' by engaging with development managers' work practices as well as providing thematic and conceptual understandings of the arenas in which their work was being carried out, whether in development organizations, government-related bodies or private enterprises. The study programmes were thus part-time and mostly organized through distance learning. They included a mixture of UK and Southern African programmes, and the experiences of over 200 development managers and a proportion of their line managers, in the UK, Zimbabwe and South Africa. The course participants were mostly between 20 and 50 years of age, and were middle and senior managers in their organizations. Over half worked in NGOs and state organizations, while a substantial minority were employed in the private sector. The kinds of activity they were involved in included emergency relief, community development, public services, lobbying, advocacy, training and capacity building, innovation and problem solving, and research and publication. These development managers were respondents in a survey carried out by each of the educational institutions (they are simply referred to as the development managers or course participants in what follows). Eighteen of them became the subjects of more in-depth case studies, which also examined wider impacts in their organizations.

The questions about today's development professionals posed by Kothari suggest that we first need to examine people's motivations for studying; their learning experiences; and the practical uses that resulted. From this survey we found that, while most development managers were studying for personal and professional development reasons, there were of course concerns to improve or change careers. As in any field of work, progression and advancement are key incentives for those working in development. However, the survey results for how development managers thought they had been helped by their studies suggest much more than a technical (and possibly even more than a hermeneutic) interest. The highest scores were given for mental stimulation, personal growth, learning new concepts and frameworks, encountering new ideas and practices, and being encouraged to have an attitude of self-development. This last is an element of the reflexivity needed both in doing better and doing differently, and the survey showed that development managers experienced a growth in awareness of ways of thinking and doing.

We used Entwistle's categories of surface, strategic and deep learners to gauge the extent of this apparent engagement with self-conscious and reflexive learning. In educational terms, while surface learners reproduce knowledge and information, 'strategic' learners are those who wish to achieve and direct their study to performing well, while 'deep' learners are those who reflect on the content and process of study to bring together overall meanings and relationships (Atkins *et al.*, 2002: 126). To what extent did such approaches to learning amongst these development managers correlate with their approaches to work? While it was found that development managers who reflected positive engagement with their work also tended to be 'deep' and 'strategic' learners, the two categories are not mutually exclusive and, in practice, participants often adopted different approaches to studying within a given context or course. It was the deep and strategic (as opposed to surface) learners, however, who felt that they had been able to apply their learning in practical terms in the workplace.

But what did this really mean? How did course participants think they had changed? And were they doing things differently – or simply better? From the survey results, much of the learning seemed oriented to doing things better. Thus a high percentage of development managers (over 70 per cent) thought they were performing better in their work: they had become more reflective than previously, made more decisions, put forward ideas more, took more responsibility, and investigated and analysed more before acting. Overall, they felt more confident. However, while line managers confirmed these results, they also noted that participants had become more reflective in general terms. Was this perhaps an indication of doing things differently?

We can gain further insights from the 18 case studies, which demonstrated several types of change,[1] including, for example, aspects such as increasing confidence to use tools, techniques and skills; exert judgement; be more strategic; have a deeper sense of perspective; use global frames of analysis; and link local with global factors in a better understanding of development. Participants also demonstrated changes in management styles:

> 'She is the only person in the organization who is willing to ask questions, to question what is going on, and to challenge management on the decisions they have taken. . . .'

> 'His first priority was to get the people on board and involved, and to help them to understand what the change was about . . . what the impact of the change would be on the organization and also . . . on the individuals in the organization.'

> 'Her primary focus is to get people involved and to do something to promote interdepartmental cooperation; she makes an effort to help people to understand what the implications of their actions or the lack of their actions are.'

Particularly important was how development managers became better able to cope with changes, either those forced upon them or those being carried out by the organizations they worked in. Some development managers were using tools they had learnt in the courses to manage change (critical use of a logical framework for designing and implementing interventions, for example, or ways of engaging in policy dialogue and policy making). There was also a more generalized effect related to confidence building that enabled participants to access and make use of the different tools and techniques they had learnt for managing change.

From the case studies, there were also some small indications that development managers were doing things differently as well as better. A development manager in Uganda, who was working in rural capacity building, took the concept of poverty as social exclusion (which she had worked on in one of her courses) and used it to persuade members of her organization to rethink its overall direction in a participatory planning workshop. She also used a course assignment on 'taking culture seriously' to try and promote a shift of thinking in her organization:

> I prepared a case study of our Association's failed Life Insurance Scheme. I attributed the failure of this scheme mainly to the fact that the elite members of the board and the secretariat staff (whose education is based on the British colonial system) ignored the power of the taboos associated with preparing for death that most Ugandans strongly believe in. This case study was circulated to our board and to our programme officers and I have, on occasion, heard them refer to it. . . . As a fundraising director, by focusing my analysis on this case study, I think I learnt a lot about the importance of being sensitive to culture as I propose or try to implement fundraising strategies.

Similarly, in the case of another Ugandan development manager who was director in an organization working with children, the case study report noted that:

> he introduced general ideas . . . which he thought could be used

in the process of developing the new country programme. . . . Some of these ideas were new to [his organization], for example the idea that development management involves external goals and value-based conflicts, and hence the need for negotiation. This led him to arrange greater involvement of stakeholders in the planning process.

These examples illustrate types of communicative action. We can also begin to see that doing things differently involved ideas and ways of thinking about development action that started to challenge the status quo or some (local) dominant truths. In the first Ugandan example above, there was even a direct challenge to historical thinking. But we cannot argue that doing things differently and challenging historical continuities necessarily go hand in hand. Doing things differently and managing change could well be a response to dominant agendas at the time, or to global forces and pressures on development organizations (for example, requiring them to rethink their priorities and processes in order to survive). We come back to these issues in the next section.

Challenges to doing things differently and to institutionalization

As we noted in Chapter 4, institutionalizing learning for development is a considerable challenge. However, whereas the North–South municipal partnerships in Chapter 4 mainly involved teams of officers, in this case the challenge is even harder as the course participant may be the only development manager with this study experience in his or her organization. In such cases, the size of the organization and the position of the course participant within it will affect the extent to which change can be effected and institutionalized. However, there are also instances of several development managers pursuing formal studies within one organization – even, in some instances, forming communities of practice.

Doing things differently involves thinking and acting in new ways that will change how individuals and organizations act on development. In other words, it involves elements of transformation and challenges to (both local and global) dominant truths. Development managers found it much easier, however, to have an effect with respect to very specific dimensions (rather than the strategic aspects) of their organizations' work: that is, particular activities within teams and departments rather than aspects such as overall communication; information management; developing systems; and contributing to their organization's mission, structure and culture. Ability to contribute strategically was closely associated with the development manager's position or status in the organization, as one might expect.

Nevertheless, there was an important shared characteristic between specific and strategic contributions to organizational change: their impact was greater if they were able to use and implement their ideas in teams and groups. While at one level this might seem an obvious result, the difficulties of working in teams and groups should not be underestimated – a theme discussed in previous chapters. Even so, with all the caveats in Chapters 2, 3 and 4, these results reinforce the idea that emerging or consciously evolving communities of practice may be able to play an important role in institutionalizing new approaches to development action, and even to help challenge and transform it.

While sharing knowledge and working together are fundamental dimensions of being able to bring about change, there were other factors that strongly influenced the impact that individual learning could have on an organization. The case studies illustrate, first, how directors of small organizations could transform structures and processes, and, second, how groups within large organizations could influence policy direction. By contrast, the isolated position of individual development managers in large organizations meant that they found it extremely difficult to bring about any organizational changes in thinking and practice.

In the first case – of directors transforming small organizations – two instances stand out. A director of a small media organization in Zimbabwe, surrounded by economic and political uncertainty, used frameworks and tools he had learnt through his studies to bring about a necessary and successful division of the organization, one which enabled all the activities to survive and to grow, but within different structures. The director of the Ugandan NGO working with children mentioned above was also able to instil a 'process approach' in his organization. In this instance, however, the director was also very aware of the difficulties:

> I am the one doing the course, the others are not, so they cannot see things the way I see them and in some cases there is resistance because of fear of the unknown.

In the second case – of groups influencing policy in large organizations – a striking case of a public sector energy provider in South Africa that was being privatized is an excellent example of joint learning and action. A group of MBA students in the organization, who became known as 'The Young Professionals', was given a special position in the organization and its strategy for change. At the time, the company was aiming to train and incorporate black personnel to take the business forward. The 'Young Professionals' reflected this policy, in turn were able to innovate, and came to be seen as the leaders of transformation in the enterprise. As noted in the case study report:

> Newly appointed young managers want to join the body and to become part of the positive work that is being done by it. Even at senior management level, no decisions which affect the people of the organization are taken without the input and advice of 'The Young Professionals'.

This last example also shows the importance of organizational environment in the extent to which development managers are able to exert new ideas and processes as a result of their learning.

In this instance, the support for formal studies was part of the company policy to bring about change in the organization. Such factors – *triple-loop learning*, or the organization learning how to learn (Argyris and Schön, 1996) – are influential in individuals being able to have an impact.

However, in the third case – that of isolated learners in a large organization – there is inevitably much less scope to influence and institutionalize change. In such instances, in spite of achieving personal and professional development, individuals can feel relatively powerless. From the survey data, comments included:

'In such a large organization, I can't really see how I could have brought about changes through the course learning.'

'I have little opportunity to influence changes in my organization.'

'I assist with staff development programmes – [the] problem is that I am not given enough support.'

The position of a development manager in an organization influenced by external pressures that are forcing change, or internally driven by an active policy of change, can lead to a different outcome, however. In the case of a large international organization based in the UK that had experienced a reduction in public funding, and needed to boost the activity of its consultancy arm to bring in additional income, a senior education consultant was able to use the course materials he had studied to set up a staff development programme. On one hand, he persuaded the management to pay the costs of this initiative and set up a peer study group to support it. On the other, he used and adapted course material to launch his own internal seminar programme with junior staff. Changes he reported included new thinking and better conceptualization of development amongst staff, and greater ability to evaluate the strengths and weaknesses of what they were doing.

We may conclude that employer support and an open environment in the organization are key factors in the effectiveness of individual learning in the workplace. Wider organizational impact, particularly in large organizations, is also closely linked to the possibilities of collective learning and action. Learners ideally need access to some form of 'learning community' to complement their interaction with their study programme, on one hand, and their organization on the other. In some cases, as with 'The Young Professionals', a group may form a kind of 'community of practice' which supplies this function. In other cases, as in the UK organization above, individual students were able to bring others into a shared learning process in their organization.

To some extent, these reflective behaviours are about doing differently as well as doing better, but much more investigation is needed to discover the extent to which they changed the nature of social engagement. From the data, doing better was the dominant story. Most participants were very aware of the technical skills they had learnt (so supporting Kothari's tools, techniques and skills capabilities critique). However, they also reported that they were able to think and reflect more strategically and could see the bigger picture much better than before. For some respondents, being able to manage things better during times of upheaval was also an important learning point. However, we would need to dig deeper to gauge the extent to which participants felt able to challenge the social relations of development and to act on that challenge professionally. Being a small cog in a large wheel would tend to mitigate against such a process (as, of course, would a curriculum that did not challenge current thinking). Thus the multiple intersections of the learning dynamics and the different contexts in which development managers work have a strong influence on outcomes of formal learning for policy and practice.

The reflective thinker and learner

A parallel story – but with different nuances – is told in another, rather more specific, collaborative study of development managers' course dissertations in which one of the authors participated (Abbott *et al.*, 2007). In this instance, the focus of the study was on development managers' reflections on their field of action, and the issues and themes they prioritized.

The analysis was framed by the debate on whether development management has continuities with a colonial administrative past (Kothari, 2006; Cooke, 2001, 2003, 2004), or whether it represents a new field of development action with a different philosophical and practice base (Thomas, 1996; Brinkerhoff and Cotton, 1999). The second perspective includes the possibility of development managers challenging and contesting existing social relations of poverty and subordination, and of becoming change agents (Edwards and Fowler, 2002). Although the development managers in this study could not be said to fall simply or directly into either camp, the interaction of their formal learning with their work led them to write highly reflective dissertations about different areas of problem solving in their fields.

Many of the development managers in the study worked for non-governmental organizations, typically informed by strong values. The reflectiveness expressed in their dissertations emerged from several areas of tension that they experienced in their professional lives. For many of them, there was a tension between 'doing the right thing' and 'doing things right'. 'Doing the right thing' tended to focus on the processes and goals of poverty reduction, empowerment and capacity building. 'Doing things right' focused in part on grasping tools, techniques and skills, and in part on using the approaches behind them. In particular, there was a strong leaning towards 'learning process approaches' to evaluation (see Chapter 1), participation, community involvement and a broad-based concern with the ethics of development action.

An additional tension related to the use of tools and techniques that often feature in organizational management rather than development management, the latter being more directed towards conflicting social goals than the former. Some development managers were not wholly comfortable with the tools and techniques either in terms of 'doing things right' or 'doing the right thing', although they accepted that the tools and techniques could be appropriated and used with other aims in mind. This relates to Cornwall's (2004) idea of contestation from within and using processes that have become part of current convention in novel ways to challenge the status quo.

Other axes of tension emerged from the relationship between development managers' learning and their focus on everyday practices. For example, they were particularly concerned with the dynamics of state and community, donors and recipients, and how to challenge power relations by building more horizontal relationships. However, this ongoing process of sense making (Weick, 1995) did not in itself result in being able to answer the question 'What is to be done?' Although individual reflection and action – more evident in a particular orientation to the world than in learnt tools, techniques and skills – suggested that course participants saw themselves as agents of change and challenge, not simply part of the status quo, as concluded in the earlier cross-programme investigation, a wider collective base of learning and reflection – or building and reinforcing communities of practice across development managers – would strengthen impact and potentially arrive at new answers to 'What is to be done?'

Conclusions: from reflective practitioner to agent of change?

Both the studies referred to in this chapter demonstrate the potential for formal learning to contribute to development: by enabling participants to become more reflective, as well as more confident about applying frameworks, processes and tools in their fields. There are several mechanisms through which this happens. For the individual, an important aspect is how formal study makes learning explicit by enabling the interaction of ideas, frameworks, tools and techniques – codified knowledge in texts – with the tacit knowledge and everyday demands of development action and development practice. The individual might apply new learning directly to a problem or situation in the workplace. However, as discussed earlier, learning is a social process that involves multiple interactions: with the text, with teachers and trainers, with other course participants, with colleagues in the workplace, and with organizational settings and environments that may or may not be supportive and enabling. There are many demands on learners: personal and professional; competition with others (either individual or organizational); wider processes that impinge on organizations, what they do and how they interrelate; and, in this instance, learning to intervene in multiple ways to achieve the social goals of development – about which not all are agreed, and around which are many conflicting forces.

Several challenges determine whether promoting reflective practitioners translates into promoting agents of change (or, as suggested in Chapter 2, combining different interests with communicative action to contest dominant truths). As we have seen above, there are a number of structural and contextual ways in which the agency of development managers is both enabled and constrained. Another key question is: agency to do what? This is where we come back to the debate between those who suggest that development management has continuities with colonial administration and those who suggest that development managers are (or can be) change agents. This debate also links back to the whys and wherefores question of Rahnema (Chapter 1), and to Foucault's regimes of truth (Chapter 2). The content and learning processes of courses and programmes in development policy and management can be constructed on the assumption that development managers are change agents, and course designers can try to ensure that the content and learning promote and reinforce reflective practitioners. In such a case, the expectation is that development managers will contest rather than reinforce dominant modes of thinking and dominant policies, when they do not meet the needs and demands of poverty reduction, social inclusion, and social engagement with (rather than social dominance of) groups and organizations with different contexts, histories and cultures. Indeed, given that difference is a rich source of learning, social engagement with difference is a key intellectual component of both formal and informal training, as we have underlined in previous chapters.

We have not really answered the question about whether development managers are structurally able to be agents of change. Given that most development managers are not directors of organizations and institutions, even though they may effect change at the micro-levels at which they often work, their ability to influence wider or deeper change as individuals is inevitably constrained (see also Borda-Rodriguez, 2008). However, much can be achieved by a group, collective or community of practice that is continually learning and contesting. It has been suggested that online communication can reinforce such processes. While the Internet is a revolution in itself, we will see from the next chapter that access to and use of online communication for learning in relation to development action still has some way to go.

Note

1 All the following examples and quotations are from the case study reports: see Johnson and Thomas (2003) and Ayele et al. (2002) for details.

6 | The Challenges of Learning through Computer-mediated Communication

Mention of information and communications technologies (ICTs) in development circles tends to spark polarized debate along broadly optimistic versus sceptical lines. These debates are usually conducted at the grand scale of globalization, encompassing economic, social and political processes and events in different parts of the world which touch us all. Our world has shrunk, and at the same time ICTs have enabled a vast and growing number of different kinds of connections in both real and asynchronous time.

For optimists, this is a good thing. We can share information and knowledge, learn together, and understand each other better. In the economic realm, transactions are facilitated across distance and are based on better information. The latter is a neo-liberal dream world of a global economy where trade barriers are being progressively removed, of markets functioning well because of the high quality of information available, and of the global spread of liberal democracy to support this economic system.

A positive view of ICTs is not confined to the neo-liberal right, however. Activists also promote the potential of ICTs to network and learn together in electronically mediated communicative action (see Chapter 2), to support and connect campaigns across the globe, and engage in public action as a kind of global civil society.

Sceptics, meanwhile, point to the digital and other divides, or inequalities. Thus there is unequal access to ICTs with the world's poor suffering particularly, either because they cannot pay or because the telecoms infrastructure is non-existent or inadequate. This is what is often called the digital divide. However writers on the subject underline the other social, cultural and economic divides which impinge on this technological definition – gender divides, rural–urban divides, rich–poor divides, age divides and so on (Heeks, 2002: 7). Of particular interest to this chapter is the knowledge divide (Chataway *et al.*, 2003: 101), which includes the access dimensions of the digital divide and a division between those who have the ability to absorb and process the information that ICTs make available – and therefore to share knowledge, learn and produce new knowledge – and those who do not.

The dimensions of these divisions and their implications for the production and sharing of knowledge take us back to our discussion of Foucault in Chapter 2. Foucault, it will be remembered, is centrally concerned with the relationship between knowledge and power. In seeing knowledge as produced by particular groups and institutions, he argues that its control by particular interests creates the dominant truths of societies. The divisions over access to and use of ICTs – although their advent in the form that we now know them came long after the work of Foucault – can thus be seen as working against those who are relatively powerless. On the other hand, it has been argued that the Internet has been a democratizing force that has enabled relatively poor and powerless people to have access to knowledge and information in ways unprecedented in the past. The use of ICTs by social movements is also evidence that the Internet is a means for contestation as well as conformity: 'the creative use of computer technology for the purposes of facilitating online protests, performing civil disobedience in cyberspace and disrupting the flow of information by deliberately intervening in the networks of global capital' (Gunkel, 2005: 595, quoted in Bell, 2007: 133). However, Bell also quotes another critical writer about the extent to which cyberculture's potential obscures 'large-scale social, political and economic developments, technological changes, and structures of power that do in fact constrain (if not determine) how ICTs are designed and used' (Lievrouw, 2004: 13).

These are major areas of debate, which it will be useful to bear in mind in reading this chapter. The focus here, however, will be on micro-level dynamics, and in particular on communication using computers and the Internet – or what is known as computer-mediated communication (CMC). Like the other chapters, this one examines the potential and challenges involved in constructing knowledge through social engagement, but this time across distance and time using electronic conferencing. We hinted at these challenges in Chapter 4 on practitioner-to-practitioner engagements in local authority partnerships, noting that e-mail was intended as a medium for keeping in touch between face-to-face interactions. Here they take centre-stage as we examine a pilot research project in Uganda that sought to support communication and learning through electronic conferencing.

Electronic conferencing is similar to an electronic forum. It may be used simply as an unstructured space for communication about a particular topic or topics. A forum may be open or closed with respect to who participates. An electronic conference is usually a closed space (although people may join or be added to it) and, as its name implies, it denotes a space for discussion and reflection. Whether such discussion and reflection take place depends on many factors: ease of access to the conference; the nature, dynamic and commitment of the group; the purpose and nature of the subject focus; the time period of the discussion; and whether or not there is facilitation or moderation.

How can electronic conferencing promote shared learning and knowledge production amongst those working in and for development within a context of the kinds of 'divides and inequalities' we have outlined above? To address this question, the chapter focuses on a pilot research project that took place in two social settings in Uganda, one in Kampala City Council (the site of one of the partnerships in Chapter 4), the other in an embryonic NGO network. It analyses the interaction between social and technical conditions and argues that, even with optimal technical conditions, the use of electronic conferencing for learning relies as much on the social as the technical dynamic.

The chapter thus takes as its starting point the digital and knowledge divides articulated by Heeks (2002), Chataway *et al.* (2003) and Lievrouw (2004) above, and examines more closely the social and the technical challenges presented in these specific contexts.

Learning spaces using online communication

A key focus for the project was the spaces within which everyday, informal conversation and sharing of experiences occur. Such reflection between colleagues is just as important to learning and knowledge production as the more instrumental practices of project design, evaluations, reports to donors, formal meetings and training sessions. In examining whether and how electronic conferencing could support such learning spaces, we tested these everyday processes in a structured setting. The technology of conferencing is more formal than everyday conversation and contains assumptions about actual or possible behaviours. These are particularly challenging if the learning community is just emerging, and if there are difficulties in accessing the technology platform.

Our study was inspired in part by recent literature on communities of practice, which, as we have mentioned earlier, divides into (1) analysing and describing their dynamics (Lave and Wenger, 1991; Wenger, 1998) and (2) their conscious promotion (Wenger *et al.*, 2002; World Bank Institute website).[1] As noted in Chapter 2 (and see Johnson, 2007), there has been considerable debate about the concept of communities of practice.

First, the conceptual usefulness of communities of practice is questioned. This critique is based on the much-debated concept of community and whether community is an appropriate term for groups, networks and loosely bound associations of people who share professional, organizational and even personal, value-based goals. Such concerns have led Østerlund and Carlile to conclude that communities of practice are 'probabilistic constructs that should not be conflated with reality' (2005: 95). As also suggested by Kling and Courtwright, 'community' may thus be 'imagined', 'symbolic' or 'aspirational' (2003: 225–6).

Second is whether communities of practice simply emerge as a historical process, or can be consciously constructed for development action.[2] Echoing Chapter 4 concerns about the need for background consensus and building shared experience, some writers have suggested that communities of practice cannot be designed (Barab *et al.*, 2003; Schwen and Hara, 2003), partly because key elements such as trust and sociability are essential dimensions that cannot be constructed by outside intervention. Barab *et al.* argue that community of practice design has to be determined by community members (2003: 252).

Third, some analysts have questioned the extent to which electronic websites and discussion fora can support learning and knowledge sharing. There is increasing use of electronic communication to promote communities of practice, notably by the World Bank Institute, although the communities in question are in many cases much more diffuse and widely distributed than those being considered here. However, Schwen and Hara demonstrate that communities of practice with the strongest sociability use online support the least (2003: 260). They thus conclude that being able to describe how communities of practice work does not necessarily lead to their being prescribed as a course of action.

This pilot project attempted to provide a platform or a technological space within which joint knowledge sharing and learning could take place, thereby reinforcing actual or incipient communities of practice. This idea is akin to providing a means for the 'conversational learning space' of Kolb *et al.* (2002), in which there are different kinds of connections that bind people together, even for a limited period of time. Such connections may include similar work arenas, whether within or across organizations;

similar or complementary skills; common commitments and motivations; linked responsibilities arising from divisions of labour or positions in different hierarchies; and shared tasks or goals. A question, then, is how and why ICTs – or electronic conferencing in this case – might support or even reinforce such connections.

The use of electronic conferencing to enhance and support learning spaces is not a simple issue: even within educational pedagogy, from which the technology was adapted (see below), online learning is much debated as well as promoted (Weller, 2002/3; Salmon, 2000). As noted by Barab *et al.*, 'Online communities are not simply technical spaces but instead are networks constituted by social and technical relations' (2003: 252). Within international development, interest in the potential of ICTs lies in the possibility of providing and democratizing information to enhance networking, empowerment and governance. But this interest is tempered by equal concern about digital divides, as illustrated in this project.[3]

Thus understanding such interactions between the technical and social settings is essential in researching the use of a particular technology to create learning spaces and support learning communities. Other literature has underlined this dimension, with respect to both forms of communication and access to different types of technology. Coco and Short (2004), for example, suggest that people engage with ICT interventions in ways that serve immediate personal and pragmatic ends. Thus they do not necessarily adopt the long-term strategic goals of those who promote and provide them. Obijiofor (1998) has also argued that communications technologies are more likely to be accepted if they do not challenge existing socio-cultural practices. Examining the sub-Saharan context, he notes that mobile phones promote oral communication and help sustain kinship relations, yet are essentially private means of communication. By contrast, the Internet promotes openness in information dissemination, and private knowledge becomes public knowledge.

Obijiofor thus concludes that the Internet as a means of communication is less likely to be accepted. These points are echoed by van Doodewaard (2006), who argues that use of the Internet as a knowledge-sharing resource in Africa is hampered by the contrast between the cultural and underlying knowledge and tools offered online, and the cultural and social realities of recipients.

So how can computer conferencing be used to support shared learning when the infrastructure is patchy and when participants are mainly accustomed to other forms of communication (including mobile phones)? As indicated above, literature in this area suggests that electronic media cannot be used to create or design learning communities: it is only possible to provide a platform (or a learning space) that will allow a learning community to emerge through its own needs and agendas (Barab *et al.*, 2003: 242). It cannot be assumed that discussion and reflection will occur if they are not already part of people's relationships and practices. In sum, learning communities can only be IT-supported, not IT-led (Kling and Courtwright, 2003: 232). These were the issues that we faced in the pilot project.

The pilot experience

The two contexts for our project differed with respect to connectivity and organizational settings. First, Kampala City Council (KCC) involved two sub-groupings.

1 Engineers in the Project Coordination Unit (PCU) who worked alongside colleagues from the Council's established Engineering Department. Engaged in activities that are externally funded, the PCU was relatively well equipped, and access to computers – for complex tasks such as engineering modelling – was well established.

2 An IT Unit was was recently set up at the Council and, at the time of the project, was in the process of installing an Intranet.

The local, embryonic NGO in Kayunga provided a much more diffuse context. This was a rural district that had relatively poor connectivity, limited access to computers, and, at the time of research, a poor electricity supply. In these difficult conditions, the NGO aimed to promote electronic communication for information sharing in relation to local development problems and was also training people, such as school teachers, in computer use.

The interest in these two settings emerged for two reasons. The first concerns the demands on local authorities to enhance their capabilities with respect to service delivery, a challenge we reviewed in Chapter 4 on North–South municipal partnerships using practitioner-to-practitioner learning. KCC (and the PCU) was one of the partners that we discussed. A particular constraint was the extent to which officers had been able to sustain communication and to share learning, knowledge and feedback about the projects in which they were jointly engaged. It was also a challenge internally in KCC – at stake, for example, was the extent to which the PCU was able to share its learning from the partnership projects and co-produce new knowledge with other engineers in the Council.

The second reason for our interest in these settings relates to how civil society organizations work with or influence local authorities in service delivery. Although we were not able to investigate this dynamic directly in this particular project, we attempted to assess the potential of electronic conferencing with an NGO whose purpose was to work with other groups and organizations in the district, and whose director had strong local authority links. Prior contact had been made with the director through an earlier research project on electronic training to promote sustainability in African local government.[4]

The project was carried out in the course of two visits and an interim period during which we observed the participation in the electronic conference from the UK. We also assisted with technical and moderation issues; we, in turn, were assisted by a technical adviser in the UK. The basis of group participation was in line with what Barab *et al.* have called 'communities of purpose': bounded groups with a shared agenda and interest in a particular project (2003: 243). The first visit to Uganda included meeting with the groups to discuss the process; asking them to agree a topic relating to their professional interests; installing the software; registering participants and training them to use it; and inviting them to select a moderator whom we then provided with guidelines on possible approaches. We observed the discussion process over a four-week period, then made a return visit to evaluate the process together with participants, using question-naires and discussion groups. Finally, we wrote reports that par-ticipants could use for their own purposes.

Using computers: Kayunga

In Kayunga, the grouping was constituted through the network of the director of the NGO. Although most participants knew each other, they came together specifically for this project. The grouping combined two people associated with the district council (an officer and the director of the NGO, who had previously been a politi-cian), a teacher, a school student and two university students. Each person had varying familiarity with computers, the Internet and e-mail. Overall, the group's access to computers and connectivity was limited, although it had more access than most residents of the area. The district council officer had a computer with shared Internet connection in her office, was studying computer engineer-ing, and was a volunteer at the NGO. The NGO had several com-puters but without connectivity at the time of the pilot. However the director had a laptop that could link to the dial-up connection. At the school, there were two computers with potential for Internet connection, but they did not have connectivity at the time. The nearest Internet café was some distance away in the town of Jinja. An even bigger challenge was the variability of electricity supply: outages often lasted for whole days at a time.

Installation of the conferencing software on the two comput-ers with secure Internet connection – those of the council officer and the NGO director – was relatively straightforward, using a CD-Rom. Registering users and logging on was less straightforward as it is a time-bound process; with the slowness of bandwidth and other technical issues, it took some time to register the participants. Logging on proved to be much faster after working hours because less demand was then placed on the low bandwidth available. An additional challenge for participants was learning the language of the software, which, like any technology, requires familiarity and tacit knowledge.

Setting up the project in Kayunga illustrates the lived experience of digital inequalities. Computers were potentially available but for varying reasons – best described as a digital poverty trap – were not usable, and communications and electricity supply infrastructures were very constrained. In spite of these difficulties the group was keen to go ahead, and decided to focus its proposed online discussion on key development issues facing the district, which the NGO director was to moderate. However, over the four weeks, a range of social and technical challenges reduced the capacity of the group to participate. All participants had substantial demands on their time because of work, studies and family. This is similar to the experience of many part-time distance education students participating in electronic conferences in the North. However in this instance, much time was spent attempting, often unsuccessfully, to access the conference rather than participating; participants were thus unable to build tacit knowledge in using the software.

Using computers: KCC
In KCC, we encountered some similar (as well as some different) issues, although in a very different social and technical setting. Three and sometimes four engineers in the PCU and two of their colleagues in the Engineering Department formed the first subgroup. Three or four people in the IT unit plus the senior engineer from the PCU formed the second sub-group. Again, they chose topics associated with their professional interests. For the

engineers, this was a road strategy policy document that they were drafting. For the IT group, it was how the KCC Intranet it was developing could best meet user needs. There was also a broader interest on the part of participants, which was whether and how the electronic conferencing technology could speed up communication between them and make it more effective. Moreover, the head of the PCU was aware of donor interest in using ICTs for promoting peer learning, and had in mind the possibility of making a case for building capability in the Council.

There were some obvious differences from the Kayunga setting. First, the location was intra-organizational, within a large, urban organization with relatively substantial resources at its disposal. Second, PCU members and members of the IT unit used computers and the Internet every day (although there was inequality of access and use among the engineers in the Council as a whole). Third, the groups had strong motives for wanting to participate and quite specific themes of immediate concern for discussion.

However, participation was also affected by time pressures and slow connectivity related to narrow bandwidth. As with Kayunga, Internet links speeded up considerably outside working hours, but expecting people to stay beyond working hours to participate in the project was unrealistic. In addition, most participants did not have computers with connectivity at home. Installing the conferencing software and registering users proved not to be wholly straightforward, even in KCC (a particular issue being KCC's firewall). Having IT experts in KCC with substantial tacit knowledge was a necessary part of resolving the technical issues.

However, there were other factors that limited participation. For example, not all participants engaged with the process in practice, even though almost everyone logged on and introduced themselves. More active participants noted that, if the activity was not part of the normal schedule, officers were unlikely to break off and contribute to an electronic conference discussion, because they are kept too busy by immediate work demands. In practice, therefore, there was low participation in both KCC conferences.

Bringing together the social and technical challenges: Kayunga and KCC

Prior to this pilot research project, our own previous experience in this area consisted of using electronic conferences to promote communication, discussion and learning in distance education and between teams of colleagues working on academic-related projects. These electronic conferences are asynchronous and thus flexible with respect to participants' commitments and place. They also allow time for participants to reflect before they post a message. However, using such conferences involves learning how to write things down in conversation, discussion and debate, rather than talking face to face. It also makes demands on participants in terms of being prepared to share thoughts and ideas, sometimes with people they have never met face to face. They thus require ground rules about conduct in the conference as well as needing to establish a basis for trust. In the terminology of Habermas, therefore, they require construction of a shared 'lifeworld' which in turn enables 'communicative action'.

In the case of distance education students, trust is sometimes based on having met each other online across several courses, or occasionally face to face at a day school or residential school. However, students' willingness to participate in such conferences may also be based on forms of expertise and life experiences that give them confidence to contribute. This aspect can lead to a small number dominating the interactions and potentially this may diminish the confidence of other participants if not properly handled in the conference.

Thus although electronic conferences can run themselves to some extent, they usually require moderation/facilitation to sustain discussion, encourage participation and occasionally to enforce the ground rules. When such conferences are used within academic study, they focus on a common purpose of engaging with learning materials and with participants' own knowledges. They can also be structured around specific activities.

These observations of using electronic conferences in educational settings formed the basis of our observations of the electronic engagements in this pilot project. As we shall see, the issues here add to the divides we have characterized above and at the beginning of the chapter, and raise fundamental challenges for technology-mediated social engagement and hence learning.

In spite of their enthusiasm for the project, the issues of power supply and connectivity, the inability to build up tacit knowledge about the software and the competing claims on people's time meant that the Kayunga participants were only able to catalogue the difficulties they experienced in trying to get their conference up and running. This result was disappointing for them even though they also gained useful information about the challenges and were able to reflect on alternative approaches for the future.

Without the same scale of technical problems, even the KCC conference moderators said how hard it was to encourage people to participate, although most logged on and read the messages. This is a familiar story in electronic conferencing for distance learning, where many participants are seen to 'lurk' (log on and read) but fail to contribute to a discussion.

Of those who did participate, to what extent did their discussion and reflection lead to new knowledge *production*, and to what extent was it directed to knowledge *reproduction* (for example, just transferring information between participants)? In practice both occurred, although the latter dominated in the short time period of this project. In the engineers' conference, the moderator began by attaching for discussion the executive summary of the road strategy document, which he had authored. One participant responded by providing comments and suggestions, but the discussion was not sustained.

In the IT conference, 9 out of 12 messages were information-seeking questions from one particular participant to the moderator about the new Intranet. However, the following exchange also took place:

Participant
As I said earlier, Intranet is a wonderful idea. My concern is instilling an e-culture. If we do not achieve that then all efforts are in vain. For example, I am surprised that I am really struggling to get the engineers onto the e-conference. If I had called a meeting we would have discussed and concluded the issues already.

Even voice communication using the intercom is still a problem, leave alone information sharing (using the network). Many times a senior official sends me a messenger to my office (or even coming physically), instead of calling using intercom.

So while we work to introduce an Intranet, we need to address this problem in parallel – getting people to abandon traditional ways and start using the new technology!

Moderator
Rome was not built in one day. Getting people in KCC to adapt to the information age may take a bit of time, but we are getting there slowly. It involves a culture change and this starts at the top
. . . .

However, do not forget that many people in KCC have gotten their hands on a computer only in the last three years. I am not saying that we should not work on the issue, but keep things in perspective.

This exchange suggests that there are other important aspects of the social and technical challenges of computer-mediated communication in organizational and institutional settings, namely the existing dynamics of communication, discussion and reflection, and whether there are any incentives to change them.

Other studies echo these findings. We have already noted Kling and Courtwright's (2003) observation that electronic discussion and reflection cannot be expected if it is not already an institutionalized practice. Johnson and Khalidi (2005) have observed hesitation to share substantive lessons via the Internet in a joint World Bank Institute-United Nations Development Programme study of the potential for communities of practice in the Middle East and North Africa. A study of Dgroups (see box on page 17) carried out by Carvajal *et al.* (2008: 76) concluded that social factors (such as cultural diversity, gender, age and personal interests) were as important as technological issues (such as connectivity and aspects connecting the social and technical, like experience in using online tools) in affecting whether and how participants used the online platform. Questionnaire data from participants in online communities parallel some of the responses we gained from participants in this pilot project. In spite of the much greater connectivity and activity of the communities investigated by Mwakalinga, there were still comments such as 'people are not responding', 'it looks like we never finish to address a topic' and 'not many people are connected to the Internet, therefore many people are still locked out' (Mwakalinga, 2005: 67).

Thus Obijiofor's conclusion that communications technologies are more likely to be accepted if they do not challenge existing socio-cultural practices also seemed pertinent in KCC. In the feedback session, participants explained the wider social context that led to a general lack of engagement in online communication:

1 There was no 'critical mass' of people using e-mail.
2 Those who habitually used e-mail in the office did not access it while away (for example, when attending workshops).
3 To the extent that electronic media (such as mobile phone texting) were used in communication, they were not the media used for discussion and reflection.
4 Senior officers in particular were more likely to communicate in the first instance with another member of staff via a secretary, rather than by speaking to him or her directly or on the phone; this type of communication added a degree of formality which was not conducive to open communication.
5 Much communication thus tended to be of a formal nature,

privileging paper over electronic. For example, paper communication was usually signed and authenticated, which in turn gave legitimacy and authority, while electronic communication did not share these characteristics.

These communication practices and the organizational structures that lie behind them do not easily lead to discussion and reflection, or communicative rather than instrumental action, and participants noted that there was a general lack of sharing knowledge and ideas. There were also gender and generational issues with respect to communication practices and using e-mail (for example, it was suggested by project participants that some council officers saw using a keyboard as women's work). For both settings, one of the biggest challenges was engaging in a communication process that made substantial technical demands, and required time commitment and changes in current communication practices.

In one sense, these points can be summarized as a knowledge divide between KCC practices and those organizations that do use electronic communication habitually and informally for discussion and reflection in and away from the office, and which have a relatively flat communication structure. Such an organization, however, is a normative ideal and probably does not exist, although some may tend towards it. 'Divide' does not seem, therefore, to capture completely the spectrum of tensions that arise in relation to electronic communication in any organization. The key point is that such communication can perhaps support but not 'be' the means of learning for development.

Reflections

We have outlined some of the debates and elements of the potential of electronic conferencing to support learning spaces. In particular, we were interested in whether this proposition could be realized in conditions of multiple social divides. Although this short project did not succeed in supporting or generating learning communities, all participants realized the potential of this kind of process and its requirements. The experience was itself a learning curve which suggests a few preliminary conclusions.

We have suggested that informal conversations and discussions can lead to learning and knowledge production, and we have asked the question as to whether such conversations and discussions can be supported electronically. As we indicated at the end of Chapter 2, the idea of action learning – or learning – spaces can capture the kind of fluid and possibly transitory arenas that may occur both in work settings and in inter-organizational and inter-collegial settings where participants pursue social goals in development. The forms of association may vary, as with the two cases we examined. A possible limitation on electronically facilitated spaces, however, is that they do not inherently imply action in the sense of enactment (Weick, 1995). Yet we have argued in Chapter 4 that building shared experience for joint learning, described by Weick as the glue that holds everything together, requires the interaction of both enactment and reflection.

Apart from the considerable infrastructural and socio-technical challenges, it is evident that electronic conferences and related e-communication structures (such as e-mail lists) can only be effective if institutionalized as part of everyday practice. For more specialized purposes, they only make sense within a set of activities to produce outputs or outcomes agreed by participants. Examples given by officers in KCC included using e-communication to follow up unfinished business after meetings. A more ambitious idea was to form expert clusters of engineers as demonstration projects of how conferencing might be used. Overall, though, these observations suggest that these discussion fora may have a limited shelf-life for any one purpose (and this in practice is how they are often used). Also implied, however, is that they are structured into something the particular grouping wishes to do (participant design). Online design, then, is about an acceptable and appropriate process of communication and reflection, not about designing 'the community'.

It is worth noting some observations from van der Velden, who has asked if 'knowledge management and its ICT tools [can] improve the sharing and creation of knowledge for development among *people*, organizations and communities' (2002: 34, emphasis in original). Her own conclusion is that social context needs to guide design; it 'should not replace but build on face-to-face meetings in which people can establish trust and relationships needed to share knowledge'. She also underlines the need for self-management of those spaces. We concur with this approach. However, even when these face-to-face facilitated preconditions are in place, there is still need for further investigation and understanding of the processes through which learning and knowledge production take place in ICT-facilitated communication, particularly the interplay between the social and technical dimensions.

Finally, returning to the discussion at the beginning of this chapter, and which links back to the big issues raised in Chapter 2, we cannot claim that any of the interactions observed in this project approached the Habermasian notion of communicative action. Could these and other difficulties faced by participants in the project be characterized as a relationship between power and knowledge, represented by the many social and technical divides that we have outlined? To this question, we would probably answer 'yes' but with the caveat that the increased awareness of the participants was also a step towards recognizing the potential of the Internet for challenging power/knowledge relations.

Notes

1   The World Bank's approach is specifically about connecting communities of practice through online discussion fora, whether open to all or by invitation. See <http://web.worldbank.org/WBSITE/EXTERNAL/WBI/>, accessed 12 March 2007. In this sense, the community

of practice identifies itself (and creates its identity) through shared engagement with the topic.

2 This distinction parallels that made about development as an historical process or as intervention (see Chapters 1 and 2).

3 Even when there is access to computers and the Internet, in development terms there is further concern about the socio-cultural bias of online information and the languages in which it is produced.

4 Electronic Distance Training on Sustainability in African Local Governments (EDITOSIA), <http://www.editosia.org/>.

7 | The Whys and Wherefores of Learning for Development

This final chapter draws together some reflections on the theories that have informed our analysis. We use the three categories from the beginning of Chapter 2 – how and why learning occurs; how learning is promoted; learning for what purpose? – to examine the nature of everyday learning for development in and through development action. We also come back to, and reflect on, the concept of action learning spaces and how it can be linked to mechanisms for reflexive development.

How and why learning occurs

In Chapter 2 we presented some theoretical/conceptual areas that are useful for understanding how and why learning occurs. We reflect on them again here.

Habermas

We noted the importance of our communicative (and hence learning) ability and the way we reflect and act on our social worlds. In particular, we focused on Habermas's concept of communicative action, based on emancipatory knowledge (that challenges and shapes society). In Habermas's view, communicative action requires shared 'lifeworlds' or shared 'background consensus': the shared experiences and common assumptions which form the basis of trust and enable learning to take place, and which might lead to 'ideal speech situations', paralleling to some extent the ideals of the participation discourse. We also argued, however, that while commonality is a basis for trust, difference is fundamental to learning. Thus both are building blocks for everyday learning.

They are building blocks in several important ways. First, in our case studies, the role of shared experience and trust was either a starting point and/or a dimension that was built through joint action and reflection. While providing a basis through which joint learning and action could take place, it also had its own dynamic. Commonality isn't a quality that either 'is' or 'isn't' – it is constructed and shaped over time. And it can also be lost if the foundations for it no longer hold or are undermined by the influence of overwhelming difference, or by external forces that are beyond the control of the actors (for example, economic and political changes that force actors apart). Equally, difference is a fluid quality within social relationships: how it is understood (as a power relation, for example, or as a source of learning), how actors engage with difference (from pretending or claiming it doesn't exist, to giving it the status of an obstacle to learning), and contextual influences will all affect whether difference provides potential for, or undermines, learning.

Foucault

Foucault's concept of governmentality relates closely to the whys and wherefores of action raised by post-development perspectives in that it underlines that different knowledges are produced for different purposes, not all of which may be benign. This perspective also argues that 'truths' can be normalized and internalized through power relations (becoming 'regimes of truth'), which, again, may not necessarily be benign or may speak to different social agendas, not all of which necessarily benefit the subjects of development. Even more difficult to analyse are the subtle ways in which learning and 'truths' may be normalized by institutionalization – which can be for both benign and non-benign purposes, in part depending on how the knowledge was produced (and for what purpose). As we noted with respect to Habermas, how and why learning occurs has a strong relationship to the kind of knowledge produced, by whom and in what way. However, as argued in relation to Foucault, producing 'truth' also involves a process of negotiation and accommodation; it can thus involve challenge and contestation and lead to learning of a particular, and potentially transformative, kind.

It is important, though, to understand the conditions under which regimes of truth – whether at macro or micro levels – can be challenged. One of the common dimensions to emerge from our case studies is the relative power of collectivities, or collective action as opposed to individual action. Examples included the pressures put on council officers and NGOs by the widows (Chapter 3), the action learning of the municipal council officers – in particular the engagement with the community on public health (Chapter 4), and the impact of knowledge sharing and peer groups engaging with formal education and training (Chapter 5). We are not arguing that all these experiences were transformative in nature – mainly they were not – but certainly the impact of the social nature of that learning was visible. And we are also not arguing that transformative action is necessarily collective – individuals in particular social positions can have a catalytic effect by bringing their own learning and understandings to bear (Chapter 5), particularly if change is being forced by external events or extreme internal contractions (the 'mismatches' of Argyris and Schön). The more common phenomenon, however, is the relatively powerless position of individuals compared with collective learning and action.

Theories of learning

In Chapter 2, we considered constructivist perspectives on learning, in which learning and the knowledge produced are the results of social processes and relationships. In particular, we focused on the concept of experiential learning – grasping and reflecting on experience leading to new knowledge and action, which may be of a transformative kind. Experiential learning involves the interaction of codified forms of knowledge – texts (from instructions and manuals to websites and books), courses, education and training – with the tacit knowledge of one's own and others' experience (for example in communities of practice, conversational learning, work teams or professional partnerships and networks). We noted ideas about how organizations learn – in particular the (Argyris and Schön) idea of feedback loops that catalyse change when there are mismatches between expectations and reality, as mentioned above. The conceptualization of how and why learning occurs is based on many kinds of difference: of expectations versus reality; of different knowledges; of different perspectives on the world. Thus a tension in experiential and joint learning is the interaction between 'background consensus' and differences between participants. A further tension is the interaction between individual or group learning and wider organizational and institutional learning, and the extent to which 'regimes of truth' and their social underpinnings in organizations and institutions influence outcomes. Many theorists have categorized learning types or styles, and we noted conceptual similarities between the types of communication and rationality of Habermas and those sometimes used in the educational sphere: surface learning, strategic learning and deep – or transformative – learning.

A particular dimension to such learning processes is the role of the catalyst – typically a teacher, trainer, facilitator, or organizer. One of the themes in the book has been the nature of agency and the different ways in which it is exerted. Agency takes many different forms and can require particular stimuli or processes to enable its realization or (Weick, 1995) enactment. One of those forms is through the roles of overt or hidden 'teachers', as in the exchanges between municipal officers or those who find ways of sharing formal learning in organizations. The role of the hidden teacher arises from a positive construction of difference – a process in which everyone can be a hidden teacher, as well as learner, in engaging with others in the world. This is of course a highly idealized account of what is possible, when in reality lack of trust and mutuality, and the many ways in which power relations within and between societies are expressed and embedded in everyday life, are a constant challenge to teaching and learning as social engagement.

An additional and challenging aspect of the social nature of learning is collective learning not to change. As we have commented in earlier chapters, this is a potential characteristic of communities of practice, and can be both an outcome of social learning (and organization) *and* an obstacle to new thinking. A particularly interesting phenomenon is presented when groups in organizations and wider society are conscious of the need to act but do not act, even to the point of internalizing non-action (which we also discussed in relation to Foucault's concept of governmentality and regimes of truth). In development terms, such phenomena present one of the biggest challenges to social change.

Action learning spaces
Finally, in relation to how and why learning occurs, Chapter 2 briefly explored the concept of action learning space, which is based on experiential learning and encapsulates those moments in which social engagement and joint action give rise to an experiential learning cycle which is the basis for further action (and potentially, but not necessarily, as we have noted, for transformative action). Such spaces may combine different knowledges and types of learning with elements of background consensus and an acknowledgement of the value of difference for learning. They thus have the potential to challenge and shape the aspects of development in which they are engaged – but as we have seen in the chapters of this book, there are many qualifiers which strongly argue against romanticizing such learning processes. We come back to action learning spaces below.

How to promote learning

As we noted in Chapter 2, in development action, and more particularly in the 'organized intervention in collective affairs' (Nederveen Pieterse, 2001: 3), there is much concern with approaches and models, particularly in learning as capacity building and in inclusive project and programme design. We noted in Chapter 5 Kothari's argument (2006) that what development professionals do can be seen as an extension of colonial administration, with an overriding focus on expertise and techniques at the expense of in-depth knowledge and understanding, and social and political awareness. That chapter focused on whether certain types of formal learning could lead to a more reflexive development professional who both 'did things better' and 'did them differently'. Although that study underlined the challenges of doing things differently, it also begged the question of how to promote emancipatory and communicative action, or to promote learning that contests dominant 'regimes of truth' and helps shape new social forms.

Contesting regimes of truth can seem like a utopian or romanticized view of the power of learning. Certainly the case studies in this book have demonstrated the difficulties of achieving joint and emancipatory learning for development more often than they have revealed the power of that process. However, the case studies also demonstrated several approaches to promoting learning – some of them deliberate, others emerging less intentionally, all of them having some value. We now consider them by using the framework of modelling.

In Chapter 1, we mentioned the use of models as learning tools.[1] In many respects, the processes we have analysed in the case studies have some characteristics of models. Models simplify reality in ways that enable us to see how it might work. Of course reality is always more complex than a model; however, the model serves to lay bare key elements around which we can then begin to understand complexity. Building models of different realities enables us to compare them, itself also a learning process. Finally, models can be built of many different social phenomena: at a societal scale (such as macro-economic models); to analyse processes (how change occurs, or how intervention might result in change; the role of participation in development); to show how one phenomenon causes another one; to demonstrate structures; and to clarify relationships (such as those between individuals and their organizations).

Each of the case studies in this book – or elements of them – could be redefined as a number of implied and explicit models. For example, the multi-stakeholder intervention of the Environmental Action Group in Chapter 3 could be drawn as a process or intervention model. Practitioner-to-practitioner partnerships (Chapter 4) can also be modelled, but one could also model examples of particular learning processes (for example around the joint learning on health interventions in Iganga or traffic management in Kampala). In earlier publications about the learning processes of development managers (Chapter 5), we have modelled the relationship between education programmes, individual learners, their organizational environments and organizational action on development (Johnson and Thomas, 2004). Finally, the online conferencing attempted in the pilot project described in Chapter 6 is itself informed by a particular model of interactive learning.

How does such modelling help promote learning for development? The first thing, of course, is that modelling is itself a learning process – by comparing models with the complexity of reality or with apparently similar processes in other contexts, one can examine the generality and specificity of phenomena, commonalities and differences, and begin to ask questions about them. Why are certain things common and others different? In what ways are things common and different? Do the commonalities and differences mean that new thinking is needed? Building models can also allow questions to emerge from theory – from Habermas and Foucault to Kolb, Argyris and Schön, and Wenger.

How can communicative action be promoted in practice? What does it mean in practice to investigate governmentality and challenge regimes of truth? How do experience, tacit knowledge and codified knowledge interact to build new knowledge in particular settings? What is needed to embed individual learning in organizations? How do the social dynamics of communities of practice promote or inhibit new learning?

The overall approach is thus not simply to use modelling to do things better in a technical rationality which promotes single-loop learning. It is also to examine the potential for doing things differently in the sense of hermeneutic and communicative rationalities which promote the double-loop learning of Argyris and Schön. Such processes require the second way in which models can be used: that is, models can also represent an 'imagined world', moving from models of 'what is' to 'what could (or should) be' – or how to do things differently. There are several ways in which models can be used to conceptualize imagined worlds: in Chapter 1 we mentioned blueprints; learning from the simple comparison of different models to build new models; and learning process approaches, which have different attributes, advantages and disadvantages depending on the settings. Imagined worlds also require ways of getting there – which in turn can involve a modelling approach.

We now add some very strong caveats and qualifiers to the use of models to promote learning for development. While, on one hand, models can seem to replace theories or conceptual frameworks (Barratt-Brown, 1995: 1), it is important to remember that they have implied theory and concepts in them. For example, the workshop model in Chapter 3 that we grandly called 'facilitated or negotiated communicative action' above, on the basis that it was investigating difference to create some (negotiated) common ground for moving forward, could also be seen as normalizing or institutionalizing truths about the place of community in public action or in supporting and reinforcing the actions of government (in this case, local government). Thus, while identifying models and the assumptions behind them is an important exercise in being able to ask questions and to share understandings, it is also essential for critical reflection on the model and on the imagined world being proposed. In particular, it can be useful for examining the whys and wherefores of development action.

There is also a tension between understanding implied models and implied theory, and proposing models as ways of promoting learning. We have already noted such a tension (although without using the language of modelling) in the case of communities of practice. On one hand, the concept of communities of practice is a social theory of learning that explains the situated nature of learning in particular social and group-based settings. On the other, communities of practice have been used normatively to propose a means of achieving collective learning and action. There are also such tensions with respect to dimensions of the learning processes we have analysed in the case study chapters. For example, in these cases of small-scale, semi-structured learning, we have noted the importance of building common projects, shared values and, above all, trust. Yet many of these processes are long- rather than short-term, and thus, to the extent that they can be modelled, they require a long-term perspective. In a more historical rather than intentional sense, they may be emergent properties of particular social dynamics over which there is limited directional control.

Learning for what purpose?

Chapter 2 raised the links between learning and the production of knowledge and what was produced, and between the knowledge produced and its purpose. An important aspect of thinking through these relationships is conceptualizing learning and knowledge as processes, not ends in themselves. Thus the kinds of purposes we have discussed in this book are themselves processual. One purpose identified is being able to reflect on the world in order to change and shape it (bring about 'good change'), accepting that there are many different ideas about what kinds of change are desired, and for what and whose benefit. Another purpose is to be able to do things differently as well as better: for example, to promote types of engagement that involve communicative or emancipatory action as well as technical and hermeneutic action; or to be able to challenge sources of power that oppress, as well as engage constructively with accepted truths. A third purpose is to be able to engage with and value difference as well as shared backgrounds, and hence to be able to engage with public action and with others in a reflexive way. A fourth is to provide the basis for changes in power relations, which are so closely related to access to and control over knowledge as well as to the purposes of, and approaches to, learning. And finally, of course, there is the ongoing purpose and process of building capabilities and capacities for further learning and innovation.

These purposes are not based on ideals simply, but on understandings of social relations and the forces that drive them, and on the pragmatics of struggle and contestation – the realpolitik of change. Yet processual purposes do not lessen the importance and relevance of doing things better as well as doing them differently. Acknowledging the situated nature of learning is also to acknowledge the situated nature of action: meeting needs requires capability and effectiveness, as much as it requires creating the capabilities and space for longer-term change.

Action learning spaces, and the whys and wherefores of development

The critical challenge posed by the post-development theorists – thinking carefully about the whys and wherefores of action – is also a challenge for the purposes of learning for development. The whys and wherefores are of course negotiated territory, and building skills and capabilities to realize better results are as much part of that negotiated territory as challenging global power relations.

We have used action learning spaces as a concept that tries to encapsulate the negotiated nature of learning and its purpose. They describe the space in which action and learning come together in mutually reinforcing form, shaped by dynamics that need careful understanding. Thus, the case studies in this book have shown that the social and technical relations of those spaces have a strong influence on their outcomes. The relative power of actors (exerted consciously or unconsciously), the types of knowledge and 'truths' and how they are perpetuated or challenged, the technical conditions of learning and action, and the way that relations and understandings can change through social engagement and contestation – all are part of this process. In this sense, action learning spaces lean on Weick's concept of enactment: through joint action there is joint learning (even if different actors learn different things); and through joint learning, there is the possibility of joint action.

We have proposed action learning space as an analytical tool for understanding the social dynamics of situated learning. To some extent, we have hinted that such spaces are something to promote. However, there is a much stronger bar to this route at present, in that we have not theorized action learning spaces as a model with particular characteristics except in the broadest of terms. Furthermore, we are aware that action learning often occurs through contestation and is therefore not necessarily easy or comfortable. Unlike communities of practice, such spaces may be quite fluid in terms of their inhabitants. Understanding their historical and emergent properties is thus as important as promoting some of the values that might enhance their outcomes, such as building trust and shared lifeworlds through engagement and understanding, and valuing difference.

Note

1 The following discussion of models takes its lead from Johnson, Chataway and Thomas (2005).

Bibliography

Abbott, D., S. Brown and G. Wilson (2007) 'Development management as reflective practice', *Journal of International Development*, 19: 187–203.

Apel, K-O. (1980) *Towards a Transformation of Philosophy*, translated by G. Adey and D. Frisby, Routledge and Kegan Paul, London.

Argyris, C. and D. A. Schön (1996) *Organisational Learning II. Theory, Method and Practice,* Addison-Wesley, Boston, MA.

Atkins, P., C. Baker, S. Cole, J. George, M. Haywood, M. Thorpe, N. Tomlinson and S. Whitaker (2002) *Supporting Open Learners Reader*, Open University, Milton Keynes.

Ayele, S. and D. Wield (2005) 'Science and technology capacity building and partnership in African agriculture: perspectives on Mali and Egypt', *Journal of International Development*, 17 (5): 631–46.

Ayele, S., P. Dzvimbo, H. Johnson, P. Kasiamhuru, J. Malaba, P. Manjengwa, F. Nazare, H. Potgieter, A. Thomas, S. Tyler and A. Woodley (2002) 'Education for development policy and management: the impacts of educational programmes on individual and organisational capacity building', final report, November. The Open University, Milton Keynes.

Baker, A. C., P. J. Jensen and D. A. Kolb (2002) 'Learning and conversation' in A. C. Baker, P. J. Jensen and D. A. Kolb (eds), *Conversational Learning: an Experiential Approach to Knowledge Creation*, Quorum Books, Westport, CT.

Barab, S. A., J. G. Makinster and R. Scheckler (2003) 'Designing system dualities: characterizing a web-supported professional development community', *The Information Society,* 19 (3): 237–56.

Barratt Brown, M. (1995) *Models in Political Economy* (2nd edition), Harmondsworth, Penguin.

Bartone, C. J., J. Bernstein, J. Leitmann and J. Eigen (1994) 'Toward environmental strategies for cities: policy considerations for urban environmental management in developing countries', Urban Management Programme Policy Paper No. 18, World Bank, Washington, DC.

Bell, D. (2007) *Cyberculture Theorists: Manuel Castells and Donna Haraway*, Routledge, London and New York, NY.

Biggs, S. and S. Smith (2003) 'A paradox of learning in project cycle management and the role of organizational culture', *World Development*, 31 (10):1743–57.

Borda-Rodriguez, A. (2008) 'Knowledge for development? Reflections from consultants and advisors in Bolivia', PhD thesis, The Open University, Milton Keynes.

Brinkerhoff, D. and J. Cotton (1999) 'International development management in a globalised world', *Public Administration Review*, 59 (4): 346–61.

Carvajal, A., O. Mayorga and B. Douthwaite (2008) 'Forming a community of practice to strengthen the capacities of learning and knowledge sharing centres in Latin America and the Caribbean: a Dgroup case study', *Knowledge Management for Development Journal*, 4 (1):71–81, <www.km4dev.org/Journal>.

Chambers, R. (1997) *Whose Reality Counts? Putting the Last First'*, Intermediate Technology Publications, London.

Chataway, J., F. Gault, P. Quintas and D. Wield (2003) 'Dealing with the knowledge divide' in G. Sciados (ed.), *Monitoring Digital Divides and Beyond*, Orbicom, Montreal.

Clark, N., A. Hall, R. Sulaiman and G. Naik (2003) 'Research as capacity building: the case of an NGO facilitated post-harvest innovation system for the Himalayan hills', *World Development*, 31 (11): 1845–63.

Cleaver, F. (1999) 'Paradoxes of development: questioning participatory approaches to development', *Journal of International Development*, 11 (4): 597–612.

Coco, A. and P. Short (2004) 'History and habitat in the mobilisation of ICT resources', *The Information Society*, 20 (1): 39–51.

Coffield, F., D. Moseley, E. Hall and K. Ecclestone (2004) *Should We Be Using Learning Styles? What Research Has To Say to Practice*, Learning Skills and Research Centre, London.

Cooke, B. and U. Kothari (eds) (2001a) *Participation. The New Tyranny?*, Zed Books. London.

—— (2001b) 'The case for participation as tyranny', in B. Cooke, and U. Kothari (eds), *Participation. The New Tyranny?*, Zed Books. London, pp. 1–15.

Cooke, W. (2001) 'From colonial administration to development management', Discussion Paper 63, IDPM, University of Manchester.

—— (2003) 'A new continuity with colonial administration: participation in development management', *Third World Quarterly*, 24 (1): 47–61.

—— (2004) 'The managing of the (Third) World', *Organization*, 11 (5): 603–29.

Cornwall, A. (2004) 'Spaces for transformation? Reflections on issues of power and difference in participation in development' in S. Hickey and G. Mohan (eds), *Participation: from Tyranny to Transformation?* Zed Books, London.

Cowen, M. P. and R. W. Shenton (1996) *Doctrines of Development*, Routledge, London and New York, NY.

Crawford D., M. Mawbo, Z. Mdimi, H. Mkilya, A. Mwambuzi, M. Mwiko, D. Robinson and S. Sekasua (1999) 'Practical notes: a day in the life of a development manager', *Development in Practice*, 9 (1–2): 170–5.

Crush, J. (1995) (ed.) *Power of Development*, Routledge, London.

Drèze, J. and A. Sen (1989) *Hunger and Public Action*, Clarendon Press, Oxford.

Edgar, A. (2006) *Habermas: the Key Concepts*, Routledge, London.

Edwards, M. and A. Fowler (2002) 'Introduction: changing challenges for NGDO management', in M. Edwards and A. Fowler (eds), *The Earthscan Reader in NGO Management*, Earthscan. London.

Entwistle, N. (1997) 'Contrasting perspectives on learning' in F. Marton, D. Hounsell and N. Entwistle (eds), *The Experience of Learning: Implications for Teaching and Studying in Higher Education*, Scottish Academic Press, Edinburgh.

Fischer, F. (2003) *Reframing Public Policy: Discursive Politics and Deliberative Practices*, Oxford University Press, Oxford.

Foucault, M. (1979) 'Governmentality', *Ideology and Consciousness* 6: 5–22.

—— (1980a) 'Truth and power' in C. Gordon (ed.), *Michel Foucault: Power/Knowledge: Selected Interviews and Other Writings 1972–1977*, Harvester Press, London.

—— (1980b) 'Body power', in C. Gordon (ed.), *Michel Foucault: Power/Knowledge: Selected Interviews and Other Writings 1972–1977*, Harvester Press, London.

—— (1991) *Discipline and Punish*, Penguin Books, London.

Fowler, A. (2000) *The Virtuous Spiral: a Guide to Sustainability for NGOs in International Development*, Earthscan, London.

Freire, P. (1972) *The Pedagogy of the Oppressed,* Penguin Books, London.

Gasper, D. (2000) 'Evaluating the "logical framework approach" towards learning-oriented development evaluation!', *Public Administration and Development*, 20: 17–28.

Habermas, J. (1984) *The Theory of Communicative Action (Volume 1). Reason and the Rationalisation of Society*, Polity Press, Cambridge.

—— (1987a) *Knowledge and Human Interests*, Polity, Cambridge.

—— (1987b) *The Theory of Communicative Action (Volume 2). Lifeworld and System: a Critique of Functionalist Reason*, Polity Press, Cambridge.

—— (1990) *Moral Consciousness and Communicative Action*, Polity Press, Cambridge.

Hager, P. (2004) 'The conceptualization and measurement of learning at work' in H. Rainbird, A. Fuller and A. Munro (eds), *Workplace Learning in Context*, Routledge, London.

Harriss, J. (2000) 'Working together: the principles and practice of co-operation and partnership' in D. Robinson, T. Hewitt and J. Harriss (eds), *Managing Development: Understanding Inter-Organizational Relationships,* Sage in association with The Open University, London, Thousand Oaks, CA and New Delhi.

Heeks, R. (2002) '*i*-Development not e-development', *Journal of International Development* (Special Issue on ICTs and Development), 14 (1): 1–12.

Hewitt, T. and D. Robinson (2000) 'Putting inter-organizational ideas into practice', in D. Robinson, T. Hewitt, and J. Harriss (eds), *Managing Development: Understanding Inter-Organizational Relationships,* Sage in association with The Open University, London, Thousand Oaks, CA and New Delhi.

Hickey, S. and G. Mohan (eds), (2004) *Participation: from Tyranny to Transformation?*, Zed Books, London.

Hodkinson, P. and H. Hodkinson (2004) 'The complexities of workplace learning: problems and dangers in trying to measure attainment' in H. Rainbird, A. Fuller and A. Munro (eds), *Workplace Learning in Context*, Routledge, London.

Huttunen, R. and H. Heikkinen (1998) 'Between facts and norms: action research in the light of Jurgen Habermas's theory of communicative action and discourse theory of justice', *Curriculum Studies*, 6 (3): 3076–322.

IDRC (2007) *Making Outcome Mapping Work: Evolving Experiences from around the World,* International Development Research Centre, Ottawa.

Inskip (1994) 'Network agents: Organisations as special facilitators of early stages of inter-organisational development' Paper presented at the Workshop on Multi-Organisational Partnerships: Working Together across Organisational Boundaries, European Institute for Advanced Studies in Management, September 19-20, Brussels.

Isaacs, W. (1993) 'Taking flight: dialogue, collective thinking and organizational learning', *Organizational Dynamics*, 22: 24–39.

Johnson, E. and R. Khalidi (2005) 'Communities of practice for development in the Middle East and North Africa', *Knowledge Management for Development Journal*, 1 (1): 96–110, <www.km4dev.org/ Journal>.

Johnson, H. (2007) 'Communities of practice and international development', *Progress in Development Studies*, 7 (4): 277–90.

Johnson, H. and L. Mayoux (1998) 'Investigation as empowerment: using participatory methods', in A. Thomas, J. Chataway and M. Wuyts (eds), *Finding out Fast: Investigative Skills for Policy and Development,* Sage in association with the Open University, London.

Johnson, H. and A. Thomas (2003) 'Education for development policy and management: impacts on individual and organisational capacity building', synthesis report for Department for International Development, The Open University, Milton Keynes.

—— (2004) 'Professional capacity and organizational change as measures of educational effectiveness: assessing the impact of postgraduate education in Development Policy and Management', *Compare*, 34 (3): 301–14.

—— (2007) 'Individual learning and building organisational capacity for development', *Public Administration and Development*, 27 (1): 39–48.

Johnson, H. and G. Wilson (2000) 'Biting the bullet: civil society, social learning and the transformation of local governance', *World Development*, 28, 11, pp.1891–906.

—— (2009) 'Learning and mutuality in municipal partnerships and beyond: a focus on northern partners', *Habitat International*, 33 (2): 210–17.

Johnson, H., J. Chataway and A. Thomas (2005) 'Making institutional development happen', unit in the course 'Institutional Development: Conflicts, Values and Meanings', The Open University, Milton Keynes.

Kelly, R. and G. Wilson (2002) Study Guide 1 to Course U213, International Development: Challenges for a World in Transition, The Open University, Milton Keynes.

King, K. and S. McGrath (2004) *Knowledge for Development? Comparing British, Japanese, Swedish and World Bank Aid*, HSRC Press and Zed Books, Cape Town, London, and New York, NY.

Kling, R. and C. Courtwright (2003) 'Group behaviour and learning in electronic forums: a sociotechnical approach', *The Information Society*, 19 (3): 221–35.

Kolb, D. A. (1984) *Experiential Learning: Experience as the Source of Learning and Development*, Prentice Hall, Englewood Cliffs, NJ.

Kolb, D. A., A. C. Baker and P. A. Jensen (2002) 'Conversation as experiential learning' in A. C. Baker, P. J. Jensen and D. A. Kolb (eds), *Conversational Learning: an Experiential Approach to Knowledge Creation*, Quorum Books, Westport, CN and London.

Korten, D.C. (1980) 'Community Organization and Rural Development: A Learning Process Approach', *Public Administration Review*, 40(5), pp. 480–511.

Korten, D. (1992) 'Rural development programming: the learning process approach' in R. Lynton and U. Pareek (eds), *Facilitating Development: Readings For Trainers, Consultants and Policy Makers*, Sage, London, Newbury Park, CA and New Delhi.

Kothari, U. (2005). 'Authority and expertise: the professionalisation of international development and the ordering of dissent', *Antipode*, 37 (3): 425–46.

—— (2006) 'Spatial practices and imaginaries: experiences of colonial officers and development professionals', *Singapore Journal of Tropical Geography*, 27: 235–53.

Latour, B. (2005) *Reassembling the Social: an Introduction to Actor-Network Theory*, Oxford University Press, Oxford.

Lave, J. and E. Wenger (1991) *Situated Learning: Legitimate Peripheral Participation*, Cambridge University Press, Cambridge.

Leeuwis, C. (2000) 'Reconceptualising participation for sustainable rural development: towards a negotiation approach', *Development and Change*, 31: 931–59.

Lievrouw, L. (2004) 'What's changed about new media?', *New Media and Society*, 6, pp.9-15.

Mackintosh, M. (1992) 'Introduction' in M. Wuyts, M. Mackintosh and T. Hewitt, *Development Policy and Public Action*, Oxford University Press in association with The Open University, Oxford.

Mohan, G. and S. Hickey (2004) 'Relocating participation within a radical politics of development: critical modernism and citizenship' in S. Hickey and G. Mohan (eds), *Participation: from Tyranny to Transformation?*, Zed Books, London.

Mohan, G. and G. Wilson (2005) 'The antagonistic relevance of Development Studies', *Progress in Development Studies* 5 (4): 261–78.

Mwakalinga, H. A. (2005) 'Are online communities delivering?', *Knowledge Management for Development Journal*, 1 (1): 62–70, <www.km4dev.org/Journal>.

Nederveen Pieterse, J. (2001) *Development Theory: Deconstructions/ Reconstructions*, Sage, London, Thousand Oaks, CA, and New Delhi.

Nonaka, I. (1994) 'A dynamic theory of organisational knowledge creation', *Organisational Science*, 5 (1): 14–37.

Noxolo, P. (2006) 'Claims: a postcolonial geographical critique of "partnership" in Britain's development discourse', *Singapore Journal of Tropical Geography*, 27: 254–69.

Obijiofor, L. (1998) 'Africa's dilemma in the transition to the new information and communication technologies', *Futures*, 30 (5): 453–62.

Østerlund, C. and P. Carlile (2005) 'Relations in Practice: Sorting through Practice Theories on Knowledge Sharing in Complex Organisations', *The Information Society*, 21 (2): 91–107.

Pasteur, D. (1998) *An Evaluation of the Uganda Decentralised Development Co-operation Project*, mimeo, May.

Pretty, J. N., I. Guijt, J. Thompson and I. Scoones (1995) *Participatory Learning and Action: a Trainer's Guide*, IIED, London.

Rahnema, M. (1997) 'Towards post-development: searching for signposts, a new language and new paradigms' in M. Rahnema and V. Bawtree (eds), *The Post-Development Reader*, Zed Books, London.

Rahnema, M. and V. Bawtree (eds) (1997) *The Post-Development Reader*, Zed Books, London.

Robinson, D., T. Hewitt and J. Harriss (eds) (2000) *Managing Development: Understanding Inter-Organizational Relationships*, Sage in association with The Open University, London, Thousand Oaks, CA, and New Delhi.

Rondinelli, D. (1993) *Development Projects as Policy Experiments*, Routledge, London.

Rossiter, J. (2000) 'Global links for local democracy', report for One World Action, mimeo.

Rowlands, J. (1997) *Questioning Empowerment: Working with Women in Honduras*, Oxfam, Oxford.

Salmon, G. (2000) *E-Moderating: the key to teaching and learning online*, Kogan Page, London.

Samoff, J. and N. P. Stromquist (2001) 'Managing knowledge and storing wisdom? New forms of foreign aid?', *Development and Change*, 32: 631–56.

Schön, D. (1983) *The Reflective Practitioner: How Professionals Think in Action*, Basic Books, New York, NY.

Schumacher, E. (1974) *Small is Beautiful: a Study of Economics as if People Mattered*, Abacus Books, London.

Schwen, T. and N. Hara (2003) 'Community of practice: a metaphor for online design?', *The Information Society*, 19 (3): 257–70.

Senge, P. M. (1990) *The Fifth Discipline: the Art and Practice of the Learning Organisation*, Century Business, London.

Smelser, N. J. (1968) 'Toward a theory of modernisation' in N. J. Smelser (ed.), *Essays in Sociological Explanation*, Prentice-Hall, Englewood Cliffs, NJ.

Stiglitz, J. (1999) 'Scan globally, reinvent locally: knowledge, infrastructure and the localization of knowledge', keynote address, First Global Development Network Conference, Bonn, December (mimeo).

The Shorter Oxford English Dictionary (SOED) (1965) Third Edition (prepared by W. Little, H. W. Fowler and J. Coulson), Volume I, A–M, Clarendon Press, Oxford.

Thomas, A. (1996) 'What is development management?', *Journal of International Development*, 8 (1): 95–100.

—— (2000) 'Meanings and views of development', in T. Allen and A. Thomas (eds), *Poverty and Development into the Twenty-first Century*, The Open University in association with Oxford University Press, Oxford, pp. 23–48.

van Doodewaard (2006) 'Online knowledge sharing tools: any use in Africa?', *KnowledgeManagement for Development Journal*, 2 (3): 40–7, <*www.km4dev.org/journal*>.

Vangen, S. and C. Huxham (2003) 'Nurturing collaborative relations: building trust in interorganisational collaboration', *The Journal of Applied Behavioral Science*, 39 (1): 3–31.

Velasco, C. (2009) 'Networks for agricultural innovation in response to market opportunities and poor farmers' needs', The Open University, mimeo.

Weick, K. (1995). *Sensemaking in Organizations*, Sage, London, Thousand Oaks, CA and New Delhi.

Weller, M. J. (2002/2003) *Delivering Learning on the Net: the why, what and how of online education*, London, RoutledgeFalmer.

Wenger, E. (1998) *Communities of Practice: Learning, Meaning, and Identity*, Cambridge University Press, Cambridge.

Wenger, E., R. McDermott and W. M. Snyder (2000) *Cultivating Communities of Practice: a Guide to Managing Knowledge*, Harvard Business School Press, Boston, MA.

Wijayaratna, C. M. and N. Uphoff (1997) 'Farmer organization in Gal Oya: improving irrigation management in Sri Lanka' in A. Krishna, N. Uphoff and M. Esman (eds), *Reasons for Hope: Instructive Experiences in Rural Development*, Kumarian Press, West Hartford, CN.

Wilson, G. (2006) 'Beyond the technocrat? The professional expert in development practice', *Development and Change*, 37 (3): 501–23.

—— (2007) 'Knowledge, innovation and re-inventing technical assistance for development', *Progress in Development Studies*, 7 (3): 183–99.

World Bank (1998) *Knowledge for Development*, World Development Report 1998/9, Oxford University Press, Oxford.

—— (2003) *Making Services Work for Poor People*, World Development Report 2004, Oxford University Press and World Bank, New York, NY.

Wuyts, M. (1992) 'Deprivation and public need' in M. Wuyts, M. Mackintosh and T. Hewitt, *Development Policy and Public Action*, Oxford University Press in association with The Open University, Oxford.

Young, M. (2004) 'Conceptualizing vocational knowledge: some theoretical considerations' in H. Rainbird, A. Fuller and A. Munro (eds), *Workplace Learning in Context*, Routledge, London.

Index